Assessing and Teaching Beginning Readers

A Picture is Worth 1000 Words

David M. Matteson
Deborah K. Freeman

With a Foreword by Margaret E. Mooney

Richard C. Owen Publishers, Inc.
Katonah, New York

Library of Congress Cataloging-in-Publication Data

Matteson, David M.
  Assessing and teaching beginning readers : a picture is worth 1000 words / David M. Matteson, Deborah K. Freeman ; with a foreword by Margaret E. Mooney.
      p. cm.
  Summary: "The Early Literacy Reading Continuum helps prekindergarten and kindergarten teachers use observation of students' interactions with texts and oral language to plan for and monitor reading development and meet district and state early literacy objectives within a developmental framework"—Provided by publisher.
  Includes bibliographical references and index.
  ISBN-13: 978-1-57274-862-0 (pbk.)
  ISBN-10: 1-57274-862-1 (pbk.)
  1. Reading (Preschool) 2. Reading (Kindergarten) I. Freeman, Deborah K. II. Title.
  LB1140.5.R4M38 2006
  372.4—dc22   2006012755

Richard C. Owen Publishers, Inc.
PO Box 585
Katonah, NY 10536
914-232-3903; 914-232-3977 fax
www.RCOwen.com

Acquisitions Editor: Darcy H. Bradley
Production Manager: Kathleen A. Martin
Copy Editor: Amy J. Finney

Printed in the United States of America

9   8   7   6   5   4   3   2   1

Dedication

To the most important people in my life—my father John, my wife Angela, my daughter Kerra, my sons Nicholas and Colin, my brother Brian, and my best friend Nancy Frazier. Your impact on my life has made everything possible. Thank you.

David

To my family

—Mother, the love and respect that I have for children and for reading was inspired by you. The times you spent reading to me are among my fondest childhood memories. I know that it is hard for you to remember, but I will never forget.

—Angel, thank you for continuing the legacy of respecting children and of reading to Emily and Luke. You are a mother's dream come true.

—Danny, you have a gift of ministering to and teaching young children. Your entrance into the teaching profession blesses me greatly. I love you!

—Ken, your support is always invaluable!

Deb

About the Cover

Colin was born with a congenital vision impairment called achromatopsia. With achromatopsia, there are few or no cones in the retina. Cones are responsible for color vision and visual acuity in bright light. As a result, Colin is colorblind and photophobic (light sensitive) and has reduced central vision. Colin's visual acuity is approximately 20/200. (A person is considered legally blind at 20/100.) When Colin's parents received a tentative diagnosis at about three and a half months of age, they knew that books would be the best way to bring the world close enough for Colin to see.

From birth, Colin was read to. He spoke clearly at an early age. Colin's first two-word phrase was "Brown Bear" (from the book by Bill Martin, Jr.). By two years of age (the photos on the cover and title page), Colin understood that reading the title on the cover of a book and on the title page was just how books were read. He understood that the pictures in a book would help him tell a story. Playing at reading was an integral part of his early literacy development and was nurtured every step of the way.

Currently, at age ten, Colin scores at the top of his class in reading and is in an advanced reading program within his school. He still loves to look at the early videos of himself "reading." He always asks, "Mom, do you think many other kids were reading when they were two?"

Contents

Foreword by Margaret E. Mooney   vii

Preface   ix

Acknowledgments   xv

Chapter 1   Comprehension for Beginning Readers   1

Chapter 2   The Role of Demonstration   11

Chapter 3   The Classroom Library   27

Chapter 4   Reading Narrative Texts   37

Chapter 5   Reading Expository Texts   53

Chapter 6   Small Group Reading Instruction   67

Chapter 7   The Interrelatedness of Reading
                and Writing   87

Chapter 8   Monitoring Reading Behavior   99

Chapter 9   Collecting and Using the Data   113

Appendix   The Early Literacy Continuum for Reading   125

References   129

Index   133

Foreword

"The foundations of literacy are laid in the early years" (Ministry of Education 1985) has long been a guiding principle of all stakeholders in the education of beginning readers and writers. Unfortunately, the understanding that "playing at reading" is an essential component of those foundations does not always receive the same endorsement.

Playing is exploring through participating, and playing at reading is an active and continuous to-ing and fro-ing of discovery and confirmation among author, illustrator, and child, and ideally, frequently among author, illustrator, child, and caregiver. The author and the illustrator spark the child's interest, igniting conversation as the child talks in narrative, as he has seen his caregivers do during shared storytimes. Each time the child returns to the book, he anticipates the conversation, developing his understanding of the constancy of story. As repeated readings increase memory of detail, he begins to understand the constancy of language and text. When the caregiver joins in the conversation, the exploration can be taken to another level, acknowledging the child as a reader. The author's vocabulary and turn of phrase can be introduced into the conversation, the child's attention drawn to unnoticed illustrative details, and the caregiver's voice convey excitement and anticipation. Every such encounter increases the child's understanding that a good book is a good book is a good book . . .

In *Assessing and Teaching Beginning Readers: A Picture is Worth 1000 Words,* David Matteson and Deborah Freeman have given us a good book. Its thought-provoking commentary on the authentic conversations between children and authors, enhanced by dialogue with caregivers, will bring readers to new levels of understanding about the nature and benefits of playing at reading. I commend this good book to your reading and reflection.

Margaret E. Mooney

Preface

We have written this book primarily for educators who are interested in developing their understandings of beginning reading behavior and this behavior's impact on literacy instruction in early primary classrooms. Moreover, this book is for teachers, administrators, and parents who know that young children have a great capacity to learn and want to learn more about developmentally appropriate teaching practices that support their students' learning. While inservice teachers are the primary audience for this book, it is recommended as a professional development resource for preservice educators who hope to teach in prekindergarten, kindergarten, and first grade.

In our first book, *Assessing and Teaching Beginning Writers: Every Picture Tells a Story* (Matteson and Freeman 2005), the focus was on developing the student as a writer. This book focuses on developing the student as a reader. Oral language continues to be an emphasis in our work. Just as in writing, a student's control of oral language and attention to picture detail build the strong foundation for a child's later literacy experiences in learning to read. While the oral language connection in our first book was to the drawings that children created, the oral language connection in this book is to the illustrations within books that children are reading. As we worked with teachers and taught in early childhood classes, we were confident that the Early Literacy Continuum for Writing was helping teachers to be more intentional in their assessing, planning, and teaching of writing. During our continued work with teachers, it became apparent that a tool was needed to help teachers as they worked with students in reading. We wanted to create a companion tool that would help them be more intentional in their assessing, planning, and teaching of reading and would complement and mirror the continuum we had developed for writing. The Early Literacy Continuum for Reading was created to fill that need. The structure or framework for each continuum is similar. It presents levels of Student's Oral Language, Student's Book-Handling Skills (referred to as Student's Work in the Writing Continuum), and Teaching Objectives. This Early Literacy Continuum for Reading will also support district curriculum developers, as it is an easy and convenient way to structure district or state early literacy objectives within an organized and developmental framework.

HOW THE CONTINUUM WAS DEVELOPED

After the completion of our first book, we were approached by many teachers who made comments such as: "Now that I am using the continuum for writing, I feel more confident in my teaching, and I can really see how it supports the growth of my students in writing—but what about reading? I wish I had something like this that I could use to assess reading with my younger students. I am using bits and pieces from several different assessments, but they were originally designed for older students. In most cases, these assessments don't have an oral language component. As an early childhood educator I know that developing my students' oral language abilities is important, and I want to use an assessment that helps me do that." As a result of that statement and many more with a similar theme, we began to observe students as they played at reading.

As we observed young students at work with books and other written text, we considered that in light of the characteristics of emergent readers (Mooney 1988). We noticed and began to categorize the similarities among students as they used the pictures in books to tell stories. Two categories became evident—how students handled the books they were reading and their ability to tell a story. With regard to their book-handling skills, some students randomly flipped through books and did not display an understanding of basic concepts about print such as book position or the directionality of pictures and print. Other students appeared to understand the basic concepts of book position and directionality of picture and print, but did not seem to spend enough time with the book to grasp the story line. There were others who had fairly well-developed concepts about print, but they did not notice the detail within the pictures that was critical to the story line. Once students had a firm grasp of book-handling skills and attended to the detail that was critical to the story, their behaviors could be further categorized into those who completely ignored the print and those who attended to some of the print on the page.

Our observations also gave us insight into a student's ability to tell a story through using pictures or illustrations. These observations revealed that some students did not converse about the book. They also revealed students who simply labeled objects within the illustrations. These students could be further divided into two groups: those who seemed unsure and used inconsistent word choices during continued reading and those who labeled objects and used language that remained constant during continued reading. The fourth group of students went beyond labeling objects and began to tell a story as a result of the teacher's questioning. The final group of students seemed to understand that each page was part of a whole. Each told a cohesive story that flowed from page to page. It was by analyzing these observations that we were able to create the Early Literacy Continuum for Reading for prekindergarten, kindergarten, and first grade teachers—a tool that would help them focus their observations and as a result focus their reading instruction.

HOW TO USE THIS BOOK

Unlike student writing or drawing, which produces an artifact, teachers can't hold on to a child's attempts at reading. In *Assessing and Teaching Beginning Writers* (Matteson and Freeman 2005) there are several examples of student writing, as well as student stories. These examples help teachers understand how the writing continuum works. In this book there are several transcriptions of learning opportunities intended to help our readers understand how the reading continuum works. These transcripts or vignettes are of actual children or teachers and children working together, not made-up scenarios. Danessa was videotaped by her parents for us. Danny was videotaped by his teacher while he was spending free choice time in the classroom library. The reading demonstration using the book *Hug* (Alborough 2000) was supplied by a teacher who shared a transcript of her teaching and discussed with us the rationale for her actions. The small group reading instruction example using *Best Friends* (Cox 1999) was taken from a video made for training purposes. These vignettes are contained within Chapters 2 through 8, which help explain the significance of the reading behaviors demonstrated by the children and/or teachers. These chapters are a mix of theory (the "why") and application (the "how"). In each and every vignette presented, we hope that you will ask *yourself* why and how practices such as these should and could be implemented within your classroom or district. These vignettes are meant to clarify the premise of this book, which is set out in Chapter 1—that *comprehension* is the basis of beginning reading, not letters, sounds, words, or sentences.

Chapter 9 shows how one district's preschool program is using the reading continuum to guide their practices and monitor the progress of their learners. This closing chapter is meant to support teachers in understanding the importance of monitoring and recording and its role in encouraging more developmentally appropriate practices described in this book. Every practice shown and advocated within this book is important in managing and creating successful early primary classrooms. It is our desire that you apply what you learn here and that your students benefit greatly from your efforts.

Acknowledgments

This book would not be possible without the hard work of the teachers and administrators from Colorado's Aurora Public Schools. We want to express our sincere thanks and gratitude to superintendent Bob Adams and assistant superintendent Debbie Backus, whose vision that assessment drives practice at every level of their district has made the creation of this book possible. By supporting the use of the Early Literacy Continuum for Writing and the development of the Early Literacy Continuum for Reading, not only have they proven that they believe assessment drives practice, but that they believe authentic and developmentally appropriate assessments give a teacher the most valuable and useful information possible on which to base instruction.

We want to thank the administrative team of the Early Childhood Education Program from Aurora Public Schools, Straz Strzalkowski, Marcia Faust-Haxby, and Maureen Gurrini, for creating a culture of learning within their school—not only for the children but for the teachers who work with those children. In using the Early Literacy Continuum for Writing and then supporting the development and use of the Early Literacy Continuum for Reading, they have transformed a typical preschool setting into a professional development environment that fosters an understanding of child development, literacy learning, and assessment and evaluation. As a result of this work, this administrative team created broad goals that helped shape their school's transformation and that they continue to use as a guide for many aspects of their program.

We think these broad goals are a wonderful example of what teachers and districts can do when developing an understanding of early primary classrooms using the Early Literacy Continuum for Writing and the Early Literacy Continuum for Reading:

- Oral language and attention to detail is necessary in the development of beginning readers and writers.
- Oral language and attention to detail build the foundation for later literacy experiences.
- Assessment and evaluation in reading and writing need to support the development of oral language and attention to detail.
- Assessment of oral language and attention to detail needs to be collected in an ongoing and systematic way in order to measure student achievement in reading and writing.
- Evaluating student oral language and student work in reading and writing is imperative to the development of students and teachers.

Special thanks goes out to the preschool demonstration teachers of Aurora Public Schools—Sandy Fermo, Sheila Dailey, Fran May, Sue Nye, and Debbie Trafton. The capacity of this preschool to develop in-depth understandings about early primary teaching and learning is in no small part due to their positive outlook and influence among their peers. These demonstration teachers are learners who have been willing to take risks and unafraid to share what they have learned. It is their in-depth understanding of the Early Literacy Continuum for Writing that has made all the difference to the success of the Early Literacy Continuum for Reading, both in the writing of this book and for its use within the Aurora Public School District.

Last, but certainly not least, we want to express our continued gratitude to those organizations and people who have been supporting our work from the very beginning. Their knowledge and input into the development of *Assessing and Teaching Beginning Writers: Every Picture Tells a Story, My Pictures and Stories,* and now *Assessing and Teaching Beginning Readers: A Picture is Worth 1000 Words* has been invaluable. We would like to especially acknowledge the contributions of the Arlington Independent School District in Arlington, Texas, in particular Dr. Jo McGovern and Lisa Strickland. Many thanks also go out to the Cartwright School District in Phoenix, Arizona, with special appreciation for Bonnie Rhodes and Maria Montoya. A special mention of thanks needs to go to the staff at Richard C. Owen Publishers, Inc., especially Darcy Bradley, Robert Low, and Amy Finney, for their support of and feedback on these projects.

Chapter 1   Comprehension for Beginning Readers

Most of who we are is determined in those first five, fleeting years of life. A six-year-old who doesn't already know what a story is will have grave difficulty in following the plot line of elementary school.

Richard Peck (2005)

Reading for very young children involves oral (speaking or expressive) and aural (listening or receptive) language, with pictures being central to the activity. In this way, the process of reading for very young children is similar to playing. Whether a child plays in the block area, the dramatic play area, or any other area of an early childhood classroom, play supports the child's understanding of himself and the world around him. With appropriate adult interaction, *play* provides the intentional opportunity for students to attend to detail, develop oral language and aural skills, develop important cognitive concepts, and to learn appropriate social and emotional interactions. The more opportunities children have to engage in meaningful play, the more the depth and the complexity of what they understand about themselves and the world expands. With appropriate adult interaction, *reading* also provides the intentional opportunity for students to attend to detail, develop oral and aural language, develop important cognitive concepts, and to learn appropriate social and emotional interactions. The more interactions children have with the pictures in a book, the more the depth and the complexity of what they understand about themselves and the world expands.

Creating meaning through problem solving occurs as students explore books and retell stories using the pictures contained within them. Just as a child is encouraged to build an intricate structure from blocks and tell a story, he or she can be encouraged to tell a story from the pictures within a book. For that reason reading, like play, can be defined as a meaning-making, problem-solving activity. With teacher support, both reading and play provide the foundation

Figure 1.1: Emily and Luke show that they understand that reading is comprehending

for the understanding that learning is meaningful and requires active thinking (problem solving). Consequently, attention to picture detail, oral language, and aural language is essential for success in beginning reading development. If students have learned to attend to and talk about the detail in their play, those skills (especially with intentional emphasis) can easily transfer to beginning reading instruction and vice versa. The better a child's attention to detail within pictures and oral language, the stronger the foundation she or he will have for reading and writing.

Comprehension is the reason we read, and children can and need to understand this at an early age.

With this in mind, we believe that it is the child's ability to comprehend, and *not* a child's attention to letters, sounds, and words, that is the foundation for reading. Comprehension is the reason we read, and children can and need to understand this at an early age. Playing at reading is a comprehension activity and a must in a child's early experiences with reading. Focusing on playing at reading in prekindergarten and early primary grades is based on the belief that early literacy instruction begins with larger chunks of information—knowing how books work and knowing how stories work. It is through working with these larger chunks of language (books and stories) that an understanding of the smaller units of language (letters, sounds, words, and sentences) can be developed. So, how does a teacher develop playing at reading in the prekindergarten and early primary classroom? What does it look like when a child plays at reading? What skills would a teacher want to develop and monitor as children read? An appropriate place to look for answers to these questions is in the characteristics of emergent readers. These characteristics, adapted from *Developing Life-long Readers,* are organized under the three broad headings of: Attitudes toward Reading, Understandings about Reading, and Behaviors as Readers. As you read, notice the characteristics that relate to attention to picture detail and the ones that deal with oral language, both receptive (listening/aural skills) and expressive (speaking/oral skills).

ATTITUDES TOWARD READING

- Is eager to hear and use new language
- Shows pleasure in the rhyme and rhythm of language
- Enjoys playing with language
- Is eager to listen to stories, rhymes, and poems
- Is eager to participate in stories, rhymes, and poems
- Expects books to amuse, delight, comfort, and excite
- Has an attitude of anticipation and expectancy about books and stories
- Expects to make sense of what is read to him/her and what she/he reads
- Is eager to return to some books
- Is eager to respond to some stories
- Wants to read and sees him- or herself as a reader
- Is confident in making an attempt
- Responds to feedback.

UNDERSTANDINGS ABOUT READING

- Knows language can be recorded and revisited
- Knows how stories and books work
- Thinks about what may happen and uses this to unfold the story
- Understands that the text, as well as the illustrations, carry the story
- Recognizes book language and sometimes uses this in speech, retellings, writing, or play

- Understands the importance of background knowledge and uses this to get meaning
- Knows the reward of reading and re-reading
- Experiences success, which drives the child to further reading
- Is aware of some print conventions.

BEHAVIORS AS READERS

- Plays at reading
- Handles books confidently
- Interprets pictures
- Uses pictures to predict text
- Retells a known story in sequence
- Develops a memory for text
- Finger-points to locate specific words
- Focuses on word after word in sequence—finger, voice, and text match
- Focuses on some detail
- Identifies some words
- Hears sound sequence in words
- Uses some letter-sound links
- Rereads to regain meaning
- Explores new books
- Returns to favorite books
- Chooses to read independently at times (Mooney 1988, 8-9).

In looking over these characteristics, the areas of picture detail and oral language, both receptive and expressive, account for the majority of the characteristics. This is evident when the verbs *interpret, retell, listen, think, predict,* and *respond* are used throughout the descriptors. A third important area that stands out for the emergent reader is book-handling skills. These three areas—picture detail, oral and aural language, and book-handling skills—should have a significant impact on the teaching and learning decisions that occur in the primary grades. By understanding these areas, teachers can support beginning readers though developmentally appropriate activities. Playing at reading is one of those developmentally appropriate activities.

Playing at reading draws upon and increases the strengths young children bring to school—their desire to talk, to play, and to use their imaginations. Playing at reading leads students to develop a basic understanding of how *books* work and how *stories* work and, ultimately, how letters, sounds, words, and sentences work. As children play at reading in the classroom library, teachers have opportunities to teach and reinforce basic reading skills or print concepts. These skills and concepts include but are not limited to:

- Reading left page before right
- Reading page from top to bottom
- Developing concepts of first and last
- Differentiating picture and print
- Differentiating letter and word
- Identifying known letters or words (such as students' names, Mom, Dad, siblings' names, or high-frequency words)
- Identifying basic punctuation (such as a period or question mark).

In addition to developing these foundational reading skills and concepts, teachers who develop students who can play at reading are actively working on teaching students how stories work. Stories have

> Playing at reading draws upon and increases the strengths young children bring to school—their desire to talk, to play, and to use their imaginations.

certain structures. These structures are made up of narrative elements and are developed through telling and/or listening to stories (oral/aural language) and by noticing or attending to the details in the pictures. These narrative elements include, but are not limited to:

- Beginning/middle/end
- Characters
- Setting
- Action or significant event
- Theme
- Description (adverbs and adjectives)
- Dialogue (speech or thought bubbles)
- Sensory detail (description that helps us see, feel, or hear).

Teachers can also use playing at reading to help students understand how nonfiction or expository texts work. Like stories, expository texts have a certain structure. Expository structures incorporate elements that are exclusive to this particular genre. These expository elements include, but are not limited to:

- A focused topic
- Titles that are usually simple and self-explanatory
- A table of contents
- Pictures or diagrams that contain supportive information about the topic
- Key words and vocabulary that are repeated often
- Text that describes the topic
- Simple endings that sum up the "flavor" of the text and connect to the beginning.

Figure 1.2: Luke shows an interest in the visual detail of a greeting card as his sister Emily reads it to him

Teachers who incorporate the instruction and practice of playing at reading into their classrooms are using the most current research on literacy development for young children. Noted researcher Marie Clay suggests that whether children learn these things at home, in preschool, or in a combination, they will be appropriately prepared to enter school if they have:

- Developed a good control of oral language
- Taken an interest in the visual detail of their environment
- Reached the level of experience that enables them to coordinate what they hear in language and what they see in print
- Acquired enough movement flexibility, or motor coordination of hand and eye, to learn to control the directional movement pattern required for reading (Clay 1991, 41).

The International Reading Association's (IRA) most recent position statement on preschool literacy states, "The preschool curriculum . . .

should emphasize a wide range of language and literacy experiences including, but not limited to, story reading, dramatic play, story telling, and retelling. There are many resources describing how this can be achieved" (2005, unnumbered). One such resource is a position statement from the National Association for the Education of Young Children (NAEYC). This position statement describes effective developmentally appropriate experiences and teaching to support literacy learning in preschool and early primary grades. These include but are not limited to:

- Positive nurturing relationships with adults who engage in responsive conversations with individual children . . .
- Print-rich environments that provide opportunities and tools for children to see and use written language . . .
- Adults' daily reading of high-quality books to individual children or small groups . . .
- Opportunities for children to talk about what is read . . .
- Teaching strategies and experiences that develop phonemic awareness . . .
- Opportunities to engage in play that incorporates literacy tools . . .
- First-hand experiences that expand children's vocabulary . . . (NAEYC 1997).

Playing at reading incorporates many of the aforementioned criteria for successful early literacy experiences. As you read Chapter 2, look for examples of how the teacher develops oral language by having students make, confirm, or reject predictions based on the use of picture details.

Chapter 2   The Role of Demonstration

Children develop attitudes about reading and writing as they hear and watch how readers, writers, and speakers think and act. Good attitudes toward reading and writing generate confidence. Teachers can demonstrate the confidence they have as readers and writers. They can also demonstrate that risk taking and approximating are parts of learning, and that—while reading and writing are sometimes challenging—it's worth it in the end.

Marilyn Duncan (2005, 130)

Demonstration is an essential teaching approach in supporting the learning of a skill at any level or grade and is the most supportive of all the teaching approaches (Cambourne 1988; Mooney 1990). The other teaching approaches—shared, guided, and independent—are all used to support student learning, but each approach respectively offers less teacher guidance than the one before it. As the students gain more knowledge about a particular skill, they need less support and the approach should change. Demonstration is typically used to introduce a new skill to a whole group, but it can and should apply to individuals or a small group whenever more support is needed for their learning.

For many students entering preschool or primary grades, playing at reading consists of nothing more than flipping through books and looking at pictures. At most, this way of engaging with books is only a surface-level interaction between the book and the reader—a somewhat passive activity that requires limited thinking. In that respect, this kind of playing at reading is not much different from that of a child watching television. The playing at reading that we described in Chapter 1 is a thinking or comprehension activity and often requires some teaching. In order for children to think more deeply about books, teachers need to consider their students' development in hearing and using oral language and noticing detail. Teaching begins when teachers determine what their students know and which approach best offers the learning opportunities their students need.

In the following teaching excerpt, the teacher has assessed her students' ability to play at reading by monitoring independent reading in the library and has decided that most of her students aren't looking closely enough at the pictures to support their ability to tell a story. She has noticed that most of her students are using just one- or two-word phrases to talk about the pictures. In addition, she has noticed that their storytelling does not connect one picture to the next. The teacher knows that she needs to model or demonstrate, in front of the whole class, how you can use pictures to tell a story. She has chosen a book with very few words so that everyone's focus is on the pictures. During planning for the lesson, the teacher reads the book to decide where there are opportunities in it to address the previously mentioned needs of her students. As she does this she is deciding what the story will sound like as she tells it to her students. She considers how she will engage her students by using storybook language, characters' voices, interesting descriptive phrases, and higher-level vocabulary.

Her whole class is gathered around her rocking chair as she begins to model how to play at reading by looking at and talking about the cover of the book. Because the teacher uses the teaching approach of reading demonstration daily—a favorite part of the day—her students take their place on the reading rug quickly. The teacher chooses books for these demonstrations that will engage her students and help her reveal positive attitudes toward reading. At each reading demonstration her students strive to be as close to the teacher as possible in order to get the full effects of the book's illustrations as well as the teacher's animation as she uses her voice and body to help deliver the story.

In the following teacher demonstration vignette notice how the teacher uses the phrase, "I wonder . . ." when looking at specific detail in an effort to generate discussion. Think about the close connection between attention to picture detail and oral language when the teacher uses the "I wonder . . ." phrase. This phrase works to draw students' attention to the significant detail within the story. In addition, notice how she incorporates book-handling skills without interrupting the flow and development of the story. For ease of reading and understanding, what the teacher says to the children is in italics; what she is reading is in bold, and the notes explain why the teacher is doing what she is doing.[1]

[1]All images from the book *Hug* (Alborough 2000) are used by permission of the publisher.

Figure 2.1: The book cover

*The name of the book that we are going to read today is **Hug**. Let's look at the cover to see if we can find out what this book is going to be about. What can you tell about how this monkey feels? What's he doing with his arms? He's saying, **"Hug"*** (emphasizing the speech bubble over the monkey's head by pointing to it). *That's what he is saying, but he's all by himself. Why is he saying, **"Hug?"** Who is he saying it to? I wonder if he wants a hug.*

Notes: A teacher's book introduction is designed to emphasize the significant information that the author and/or illustrator uses to help focus the reader's attention on what is to come. In this particular book, the significant information on the cover is the monkey and the speech bubble, which also contains the book's title. The speech bubble could suggest that the monkey is searching for a hug.

Figure 2.2: Inside the cover

Here's our monkey friend again. I wonder why he is the only thing on the page. He's all alone, but he looks happy, doesn't he? Where do you think he's going?

Notes: Every page has something to offer, especially in a picture book. This page comes before the title page and helps add to the discussions and questions that were asked previously, during the look at the cover.

Figure 2.3: The title page

Here he is again. He's not the only thing on the page this time. The story looks like it might take place in the jungle. He seems to be going somewhere. Where do you think he's going? Is he looking for a hug? Let's read and find out. The name of this book is **Hug** (pointing to the title) *and it's by* ***Jez Alborough*** (pointing to author's name).

Notes: The title page can be a place where readers get more information that will help to confirm or add to the readers' initial predictions. In this particular book the readers get the chance to confirm their prediction that the monkey is alone and might be in search of a hug.

Figure 2.4: Pages 1 and 2

As she shares pages 1 and 2 with the students, she says: ***As Little Monkey walked along the jungle path, he saw a mother elephant giving her baby a hug. He called out, "HUG."*** *I think he wants a hug from Mother Elephant.*

Notes: Because she wants her students to understand that books have a language style different from our daily speech, the teacher uses phrases such as this opening one to mimic storybook language.

To demonstrate the book-handling skill that a left page is read before the right-hand one, the teacher gently taps the left page to focus the students' attention on where to begin. The teacher has learned how to naturally incorporate and demonstrate book-handling skills without necessarily discussing them and interrupting the flow and development of the story.

Figure 2.5: Pages 3 and 4

For pages 3 and 4, the teacher reads and comments: ***He continued along the jungle path when he came upon a mother iguana giving her baby a hug. He called out, "HUG." A little farther down the path he came upon a mother snake giving her baby a hug. He called out, "HUG."*** *I think he really wants a hug. I wonder how he feels. Look at his face. Do you think he's been getting hugs? Where is his mother?*

Notes: Repetition of story language helps students anchor on words or phrases that enable them to participate in the initial telling of the story and in subsequent independent retellings of the story over time.

Figure 2.6: Pages 5 and 6

Looking at pages 5 and 6, the teacher reads: **Little Monkey kept walking.** *Look at his friends. What are they thinking? Do you think they want to help him? What will they do for Little Monkey?*

Notes: In most books there are natural stopping points that can be used to further develop the students' ability to make more meaningful predictions about events to come. By using more *teacher talk* (what the teacher says to the students during the reading) than *text talk* (the actual reading), teachers can guide students to notice details that are critical to the story. It is the teacher's tone of voice and the language the teacher uses that differentiates between teacher talk and text talk.

It is the teacher's tone of voice and the language the teacher uses that differentiates between teacher talk and text talk.

Figure 2.7: Pages 7 and 8

As the teacher shows the students pages 7 and 8, she says: *Mother Elephant picked up Little Monkey. He said, "HUG." She wanted to help Little Monkey. "Are you looking for your mother?" She picked him up and off the three friends went in search of his mother.*

Figure 2.8: Pages 9 and 10

The teacher continues on pages 9 and 10 with: ***The three friends walked and walked and walked. At the edge of the jungle they saw a mother lion hugging her babies. From the top of the elephant's head, the monkey called out "HUG."***

Notes: The teacher shifts to using more text talk and less teacher talk at pages 7, 8, 9, and 10 because the students now have more knowledge of the story and can begin to make more connections and predictions for themselves.

Figure 2.9: Pages 11 and 12

On pages 11 and 12, the teacher reads and comments: ***A little further along, the three friends spied a mother giraffe with her baby. "HUG."*** *I wonder if he will ever find his mother.*

Notes: Vocabulary development can be controlled more easily in a wordless picture book than a regular picture book. Teachers can decide when to introduce new vocabulary words. In this example, to introduce a new vocabulary word, the teacher changed the word "saw" on pages 9 and 10 to "spied" on pages 11 and 12. This kind of intentional decision on the teacher's part shows children how many different words can convey the same meaning.

Figure 2.10: Pages 13 and 14

For pages 13 and 14, the teacher says: *Oh, look at all the animals. These are all the animals that Little Monkey has seen. Look at their faces. How do you think they feel?* **As Little Monkey and the elephants were about to leave, they spotted a baby hippo hugging its mother. "HUG," murmured Little Monkey.**

Notes: The teacher looks for every opportunity to reinforce her previous teaching. On page 13, the teacher points out the critical detail of the animals' faces that could easily be overlooked by students. In addition, the teacher continues to develop vocabulary in a meaningful way—*saw, spied,* and *spotted.* The teacher also shifts from using words such as *said* and *called* to more interesting vocabulary such as *murmured.*

Figure 2.11: Pages 15 and 16

On pages 15 and 16, the teacher shares: ***It was all too much. Little Monkey couldn't stand it any longer. He screamed at the top of his lungs, "HUG!"*** *Look at Little Monkey's mouth and how big the word "hug" is. You can really tell that he is screaming.*

Notes: This nearly wordless book presents an opportunity for teachers to make connections between pictures and words. On this page there is a strong connection between the picture and the way the word "hug" is used. Should a book contain absolutely no words, the teacher may want to write a word or two on a self-stick note and place it in the book in order to make the connection between the pictures and words more intentional.

Figure 2.12: Pages 17 and 18

While showing the students pages 17 and 18, the teacher says: ***"HUG," moaned Little Monkey. All he wanted was a hug from his mother. Nobody knew what to do.*** *Do you think he will ever get that hug?*

Notes: To foster students' engagement at this point in the telling of the story, the teacher may change the position of anchor words or phrases. On pages 17 and 18 she changes the position of the word "HUG" to the beginning of her narration. In addition to the change in the location of the word, there would also be an accompanying change in the teacher's tone of voice.

As the teacher reaches the climax of the story, the emphasis from that point on needs to address the questions that are on the mind of the reader (or in this case, the listeners)—Where is Little Monkey's mom? Will his friends help him find his mom? Will he get the hug he needs so badly? How will the story end? The structure of a story is important. Teachers need to understand how a story builds, where and how it climaxes, and how a story comes to a satisfying ending. Satisfying endings, whether happy or sad, are important to readers (or listeners) in understanding that messages have meaning and touch something inside them. At the end of our story *Hug,* Little Monkey and his mom finally meet. As one might expect, all the other animals are there to be part of the cheerful reunion between mother and son. Before they both depart back to the jungle, Little Monkey turns to the mother elephant and gives her a *huge* hug for the help she gave him in finding his mother.

With the teacher content that she was able to demonstrate how a story flows from picture to picture, she knows that her students have a better understanding of the beginning, middle, and end of a story. This teacher understands that she will need to model this narrative feature and others many times in order for her students to take on similar behaviors. She understands that her students will need opportunities to practice these skills and has created a substantial classroom library that will provide the materials for this practice. This classroom library will support the teacher in assessing her students' playing at reading skills by offering a place to observe and monitor what the children are practicing and beginning to understand. This assessment information will provide the teacher with specific teaching points or objectives for future demonstrations. In Chapter 3 notice how the teacher has intentionally organized the materials and the space in her classroom library to support students as they practice these skills and her actions as she conducts assessments.

Chapter 3   The Classroom Library

A classroom literacy center is essential for children's immediate access to literature. Children in classrooms with literature collections read and look at books 50 percent more than children without such collections. The efforts spent in creating an inviting atmosphere for a classroom literacy center are rewarded by increased interest in books.

Lesley M. Morrow (in Morrow and Weinstein 1986)

The classroom library is an important component in playing at reading and thus developing reading comprehension in the prekindergarten, kindergarten, and first-grade classroom. The teacher in the kindergarten room shown in this chapter dedicates over a quarter of the space in her classroom to the library area. It is an attractive area with comfortable seating. Everything in the library is well organized and within easy reach of all students, inviting readers to stay awhile and enjoy (see Figure 3.1). It is easy to see that this teacher values not just reading books but reading as an integral part of the day for learning and teaching. The physical features of a classroom literacy center can play an important role in enticing children to use this important instructional area. As Morrow notes, "A classroom literacy

Figure 3.1: A full view of a kindergarten classroom library

center should be a focal area, immediately visible and inviting to anyone entering the classroom" (2001, 168).

In order for the classroom library to be an effective area in a meaning-based classroom, expectations are critical to its successful use. The teacher has posted the expectations that govern the behavior she expects students to abide by. Because the teacher understands emergent readers, she uses pictures and words to convey the simple but essential expectations that make the classroom run smoothly and pleasantly. Since pictures are an important source of information for very young readers, it is easier for them to access that information, especially when asked by the teacher to go over the classroom library expectations when needed, as shown in Figure 3.2.

Figure 3.2: The poster of expectations made more accessible for emergent readers in this kindergarten classroom library

Books in an effective classroom library should be categorized for easy selection (Fractor et al. 1993).

Books in an effective classroom library should be categorized for easy selection (Fractor et al. 1993). The books are organized by topics, genres, and authors (Figure 3.3). The teacher uses inexpensive plastic tubs as an organizational tool. Again, she uses pictures with corre-

Figure 3.3: Plastic tubs and shelves with labels are used to help organize and categorize the classroom library

sponding words to identify each container. The teacher places manageable quantities of books (between twenty and thirty) within each tub in an effort to support students in quickly choosing and returning books. Some of the texts are displayed with the covers facing forward for easy selection, but because of the limited space for the number of books in the library that is not always possible. Some of the books are stored with their bindings facing out; students know they are allowed to and even expected to take the containers off the shelf so they can browse books at their leisure.

The largest proportion of titles in this library, like many others, is fiction or narrative texts. Looking at the number of books in this one section of narrative texts (Figure 3.4) it is easy to see that the total number of books far exceeds the recommended 700 to 750 total suggested by Allington and Cunningham (1996).

Figure 3.4: The main section of the classroom library consists of fiction texts

Another popular section in the library is the nonfiction or informational text section. According to Harwayne in *Going Public: Priorities and Practices at The Manhattan New School,* she expects to see classroom libraries brimming over with nonfiction texts (1999). It is obvious from the amount of space dedicated to informational text, as shown in Figure 3.5, that the teacher in this classroom understands the importance of informational reading. The teacher makes a concerted effort to model and support the use of informational text so that her students have resources to answer the many questions they have about the world.

The area for the daily read aloud by the teacher is close to the library area (Figure 3.6). The teacher has a container of her most recent read-aloud books so that children know where they can access and borrow those books when they are in the classroom library. Many of the children can be found during the day sitting in the teacher's rocking chair reading their favorite of her most recent read-alouds.

The teacher makes a concerted effort to model and support the use of informational text.

Figure 3.5: Nonfiction or informational text is categorized by topic

The puppet theatre is a busy part of the classroom library (Figure 3.7). The students have access to puppets that they use to act out the stories they read or hear. The teacher sets out story characters that go with books she has previously read to her students. She wants her students to practice retelling those stories. By placing certain characters from familiar books in the classroom library, the teacher can easily assess her students' ability to retell these stories. Using characters from familiar books is also supportive for teachers as they work to help students incorporate any detail that might be missing in their retellings.

Figure 3.6: The teacher's read-aloud area and her book box of her most recent read-alouds

In addition to hearing daily read-alouds, listening to stories on tape is an essential part of the classroom activities (Figure 3.8). The teacher understands that the more the students hear stories read by fluent readers, the more the students understand what reading is supposed to sound like. Listening to stories on tape also reinforces what young children are coming to understand about how books and stories work.

Figure 3.7: The puppet theater is an important component of the emergent classroom library

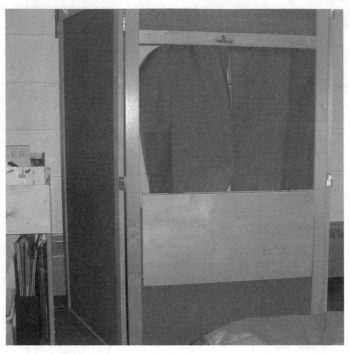

The space devoted to the classroom library, the library's accessibility and position within the classroom, its attractiveness and appeal to learners, and the number and kinds of books available to the students make a powerful statement regarding this teacher's understandings about beginning reading instruction. The classroom library's structure, contents, and use are built upon this teacher's understandings about reading and writing. She knows that reading and writing go hand in hand and that reading and writing activities must be meaningful and seem worthwhile to the student. In addition she understands that a wide range of texts in her classroom library

Figure 3.8: The listening center as part of the classroom library and posted rules that guide its use

influences even the youngest readers and writers. This teacher believes that the classroom library is an excellent place in the classroom to gather informal literacy assessments. Creating this type of learning environment takes thought and planning, but the reward is an environment in which young learners flourish as readers and writers (adapted from Ministry of Education 1997, 6).

Early childhood teachers who keep beliefs such as these at the forefront when developing their classroom environments and instruction are building the same sound foundations that literate homes build for their own children. In Chapter 4, we make connections between the opportunities for literacy development afforded young children in literate homes and the opportunities that must be available to all children in every early childhood classroom. That chapter explores the idea that given the appropriate environment and support, young children readily demonstrate control of beginning reading skills—knowledge of how books and stories work.

Chapter 4 Reading Narrative Texts

If narrative is characteristic of adult thinking, it is even more typical of children's. It is estimated that some 80 percent of children's thinking can be described as narrative. Send a naughty child to his room, and he thinks of all the places that he'll run away to, just as in Sendak's (1963) *Where the Wild Things Are*. This is the appeal of the classic story: It taps into the well-springs of all the stories that children have been telling themselves. Yet it provides a more satisfying conclusion than many of their imaginings, for it ends with Max's coming home to find his supper waiting for him as a symbol of his mother's love and reconciliation. Stories can resolve problems even for young children.

Charlotte Huck (1999, 113)

You know right away when you are in a home that values reading. Reading material is everywhere. All sorts of material—novels, picture books, magazines, newspapers, clippings, lists, cards, children's work—are in every nook and cranny. Literate homes view reading as significant as any other family activity. In homes such as these, everyone seems to be reading all the time. In a highly literate home, even the smallest child seems to be invested in reading. Bedtime stories are a sacred ritual and seldom skipped. Trips to the local libraries and book stores happen almost as frequently as trips to the market. Children's books can be found in every room of the house—even the bathroom reading compilation has books meant for both parent and child. In this kind of household, you are apt to find just as many books as toys in the toy box.

With reading experiences such as these, it is no surprise that children from literate homes usually see themselves as readers from a very early age. When young children are read to frequently and see others read often, especially significant others such as siblings, parents, and grandparents, they want to imitate those reading behaviors. For many of these young children, their reading takes the form of pretend reading. *Pretend reading* or *playing at reading* plays a crucial role in a child's literary development.

DANESSA PLAYS AT READING A NARRATIVE TEXT

Let's look at one such reader. Danessa, four years old, is the youngest of three sisters. She comes from a family that loves to read. Her oldest sister reads frequently for both herself and for school. Her mother and father both are voracious readers. Danessa also spends time with her grandparents, who are also readers. Because of the interactions of those closest to her, Danessa feels like a reader. In the following scenario, Danessa is reading to her father. As she reads, notice how she controls both the book and the telling of a story, much like that of a more experienced reader. As you read, consider the impact of beginning reading instruction that develops and supports later reading proficiency of young readers like Danessa. Think about your own teaching practices and how they directly support later reading proficiency. As in Chapter 2, keep in mind that what Danessa reads is written in bold and what she says or does during her reading is written in italics. The notes explain the significance of what she is doing as she reads.

Figure 4.1: Examining the cover

Danessa confidently reads as the title, ***Arthur Lost His Gerbil.***[1]

[1]All images from the book *Where's Arthur's Gerbil?* (Brown 1997) are used by permission of the author and publisher.

Notes: Marc Brown's "Arthur" books are among Danessa's favorites to read. Her parents have bought or borrowed many of the books in that series and read them to her again and again. Of all the Arthur books, Danessa has read *Where's Arthur's Gerbil?* several times.

Because of this, she has developed a good memory for the text and strong concepts about print. Understanding the similarities of books, especially those by the same author, is very supportive for beginning readers. Knowing how books or stories work is a desired outcome of playing at reading. Notice in the following vignette that even though the reading isn't accurate, the meaning of each page is very close to the text. Also, notice how Danessa uses expression and the story's major phrases appropriately and how effectively she tells the story of Arthur's gerbil.

Figure 4.2: Pages 1 and 2 of *Where's Arthur's Gerbil?*

Arthur lost his gerbil, repeats Danessa as she turns to page 1. She lifts the flap on page 2 and says, ***"Pal, have you seen my gerbil?"***

Notes: Books like this require a reader to be interactive. Lifting the flap creates a sense of anticipation and a stronger sense of confirmation—no matter how many times it has been read. The confirmation that occurs during these repeated readings supports the idea of the constancy of text and pictures. *Where's Arthur's Gerbil?* has a strong storyline shaped largely by supportive pictures. The text is limited and has familiar vocabulary, which increases the child's ability to remember the text.

Figure 4.3: Pages 3 and 4

Danessa quickly turns to pages 3 and 4. ***"I know where he is—in my toy box. NOOOO!"*** sings out Danessa, trying to sound a bit exasperated.

Notes: Playing at reading results in increased comprehension and fluency. During initial readings with children, discussions about how characters feel support comprehension and fluency. These discussions result in delightful retellings by children for others to hear and participate in.

Figure 4.4: Pages 5 and 6

Danessa reads on to pages 5 and 6, repeating, ***"I know where he is. Socks . . . My gerbil . . ."*** Danessa thinks momentarily about the story and states a bit more confidently, *No, it's **"my long, smelly sock."***

Notes: Playing at reading is a way for young children to experience what it sounds like to be a reader. Monitoring and self-correcting are essential parts of reading. As they work their way through the telling of a story, it is important that children be asked, "Does that make sense?" and/or "Does that sound right?" It is through these problem-solving behaviors that children come to more fully understand how books and stories work.

Figure 4.5: Pages 7 and 8

On pages 7 and 8, Danessa eagerly continues, ***"Is he in D. W.—D. W.'s playhouse?"*** *No,* she says, answering her own question. ***"So that's where all the cookies went!"*** She looks up and says to her dad, *D. W.'s probably a pig—a pig about everything—except chocolate, I think. I think she's a pig about chocolate.*

Notes: Making connections through self-talk supports the idea that this reader is making sense of what she is reading. The parent has obviously supported the child's ability to talk about what has just been read and relate it to some aspect of her life. This increases the child's ability to make connections and increase her comprehension. Danessa's use of the phrase "I think . . ." shows that she is making connections to her own feelings and understandings about chocolate—who could *not* be a pig about chocolate? Skillful readers do this

Figure 4.6: Pages 9 and 10

very quickly and almost without thinking, but for very young children this needs to be encouraged and expressed orally.

"And D. W. was in the shower," continues Danessa, now on pages 9 and 10. *"You never want to take a bath before,"* she states firmly. Thinking about what she just said, she confirms her statement by saying *No* softly to herself.

Danessa puts the book down to get a drink of water. She returns to her rocker and picks up her doll, which was sitting next to her. She says to the doll, *You can help me read—when I'm in trouble—if I have trouble, uh-oh.* She returns to pages 11 and 12 of the book and says, *"You better not be in Mom's br . . . briefcase!"* She looks up from the book and thinks out loud, *Maybe Mom has a new job.* She shrugs and confirms, *Maybe she does.*

Figure 4.7: Pages 11 and 12

Notes: The ability to make inferences from the details within the illustrations is an important aspect of playing at reading. This reader's comment about Mom's new job demonstrates her ability to make inferences. Danessa also understands that books can be read over time. She knows that she can pick up where she left off. Her parents have modeled this behavior by using bookmarks themselves and by providing them for Danessa.

Figure 4.8: Pages 13 and 14

"I know where you are. You're in Baby Kate's roll—" Not happy about her reading of pages 13 and 14, she repeats, *"I know where you are. You're in Baby Kate's stroller."* Danessa opens the flap and with a lot of expression says, *"No, it's just Baby Kate."*

Figure 4.9: Pages 15 and 16

Danessa starts right in reading page 15. ***"My gerbil's decided to get his own breakfast by his-self."*** She pulls down the flap and with wonderful intonation says, ***"No—but it's a great prize!"***

"Oh, how did you get in there?" she reads on pages 17 and 18 with some concern in her voice. ***"Oh, it's a rea . . . Oh, it's a r—reath."*** Danessa struggles to remember a phrase from the book. With one final effort she blurts out, ***"Oh, what a relief!"*** Pleased, she continues along and finishes up with, ***"It's just my shoelace."***

Notes: Danessa's parents know that perseverance is a quality that needs to be developed in young readers. They let her work on problems up to a point, but intervene before she reaches frustration. Because of this, Danessa has the desire to work problems out for herself as she meets challenges when reading.

Figure 4.10: Pages 17 and 18

Figure 4.11: Pages 19 and 20

Danessa immediately turns the flap on page 20. ***"How will I find my gerbil—how can I go to school when I can't find my gerbil?" "I thought you would feel that way, Arthur."*** With lots of voice, Danessa sings out, *It's the gerbil in his lunch box!*

She closes the book quickly and jumps out of the rocker, saying, *I'm all done, Daddy.* She puts the book back in the toy box and searches for other books. With another Arthur book in hand, Danessa asks her dad, *How about we read this one?*

TALKING WITH CHILDREN ABOUT STORIES

Even though Danessa is four years old, she still has over eighteen months before she enters kindergarten. Why is she able to play at reading so effectively? How has Danessa come to understand how books and stories work? How will what she knows impact her kindergarten achievement and future reading and writing experiences? How can early childhood teachers recreate the literate atmosphere that allowed Danessa to develop her understandings of how books and stories work?

Parents in literate homes read often. Among parents who read frequently read a wide variety of literature, novels are a large component of their reading. As a result, they have a strong internalized understanding of narrative texts. This understanding of narrative texts easily transfers to the statements they make, the conversations they have, and the questions they ask their children about the picture books they read together. These statements, conversations, and questions usually focus on the following elements of narrative texts that are found in novels and children's books alike. These elements include but are not limited to:

- Beginning/middle/end
- Characters
- Setting
- Action or significant event
- Theme
- Description (adverbs and adjectives)
- Dialogue (speech or thought bubbles)
- Sensory detail (description that helps us see, feel, or hear).

In Danessa's house it is not uncommon to hear her parents talk about the characters or the setting in the stories they read with her. They often comment on how mean or nice or pretty or handsome the heroes or villains are. It is not unusual to hear descriptive phrases like "shaking in their boots" or story language like "in a deep, dark forest" borrowed from the other books they have read. In doing so, they are using description and sensory detail in an attempt to elicit an emotional response. This emotional response is evidence that young readers are making connections to the text or anticipating what's to come. Parents or caregivers like Danessa's love to see reactions from their children as the plot unfolds, just as their teachers will. They love to see their faces as they discover at the end of the story that the lost children are joyously reunited with their families or that the villains get their just rewards for their dastardly deeds. It is story themes such as these that not only support children's feelings that all is well in their world but help them to come to understand the world.

In today's busy world it seems we make fewer opportunities to read books or other kinds of texts. In families with different values about or emphasis on literacy, many young children don't have the kind of solid foundation needed to learn easily in school and other learning situations. In order to build a foundation that is both academically rigorous and developmentally appropriate, it more important than ever that early primary educators understand the role that playing at reading and other skills of literacy can contribute to developing those beginning reading skills.

Early childhood teachers need to understand and incorporate elements of narrative texts in their teaching, explicitly recreating these same kinds of interactions that seemingly occur so naturally in literate homes.

As mentioned in Chapter 1, *comprehension* is the reason we read, and children can and need to understand this at an early age. In an effort to achieve this goal, early childhood teachers need to understand and incorporate elements of narrative texts in their teaching, explicitly recreating these same kinds of interactions that seemingly occur so naturally in literate homes. These supportive literacy interactions are developed through the kinds of teaching approaches described in this book—demonstrations, small group instruction, and individual practice. It is also developed through the classroom structures put into place that focus on literacy development, such as the classroom library. Prekindergarten and early primary teachers who understand the elements of narrative texts and use them to develop solid literacy foundations will set the stage for later formal reading instruction. Whether their later reading instruction deals with learning how letters, sounds, words, and sentences work or with more in-depth comprehension instruction such as inferencing, students who understand narrative elements early on will be freed up to focus on these skills and others that will further develop their reading proficiency without sacrificing comprehension.

Knowing how books and stories work doesn't apply just to narrative texts. Expository texts have a structure, and young children need to experience playing at reading using this genre as well. Chapter 5 looks at how one kindergarten teacher tried to shift his instruction from using primarily narrative texts to developing his students' understandings of how informational texts work.

Chapter 5 Reading Expository Texts

When children's reading preference is for narrative, they fit well with the typical text offerings of early childhood classrooms. When their choice preference is informational, children fit considerably less well. For children at risk for or struggling with learning to read, there is particular reason to pay attention to research on reading interest and preference. Interest has an important influence on children's enthusiasm and can even support children's reading development.

Nell Duke (2003, 15)

Danny, a kindergartner, finished writing in his journal earlier this morning. His teacher published the story he wrote in a small book for Danny to illustrate and to read and re-read on his own. Now the teacher asks him to check his planning sheet to see what's next on his list of classroom activities. Danny sees the classroom library is next on his list and promptly sets off for his favorite activity—exploring books in the classroom library. Like many of the other children in this classroom, Danny has a wide variety of interests, and the informational section of the classroom library is his usual stop. His teacher has worked hard to increase his selection of informational books in the classroom library due to his school's focus on using more informational text with students. After his school faculty read Nell Duke's article, "The Case for Informational Text" in *Educational Leadership* (2004), Danny's teacher set out to incorporate the four strategies Duke describes to improve informational comprehension:

- Increase students' access to informational text
- Increase the time students spend working with informational text in instructional activities
- Explicitly teach comprehension strategies
- Create opportunities for students to use informational text for authentic purposes (Duke 2004).

The teacher found that many of his students were playing at reading when it came to stories but were not as confident when it came to playing at reading informational text.

Expanding the informational section of his classroom library was one way to meet Duke's strategies in his classroom, but Danny's teacher also needed to look at how his students were using those informational texts. Because the focus in his school had been on narrative texts, the teacher found that many of his students were playing at reading when it came to stories but were not as confident when it came to playing at reading informational text. Now that the school's focus had turned to informational text he knew he needed to model that for them, but wondered if he knew enough about how informational texts worked and sounded like at this level to do so. Danny's teacher looked over many informational texts across different levels to see how they are structured and what he might use to help his students begin to better understand this genre. In his search he found that there were many commonalities in the features of those texts that he could use to support himself as he modeled. Knowledge of these common expository features would support his students in playing at reading in this genre. From that investigation the teacher produced this list:

- A focused topic
- Titles that are usually simple and self-explanatory
- A table of contents
- Pictures or diagrams that contain supportive information about the topic
- Key words and vocabulary that are repeated often
- Text that describes the topic
- Simple endings that sum up the "flavor" of the text and connect to the beginning.[1]

Over the next few weeks Danny's teacher used his new understandings and demonstrated what it looked and sounded like to play at reading using informational texts. All of his teaching points or objectives in these reading demonstrations were from the list of elements he formulated from looking at informational texts. During that time Danny's teacher monitored his students' use of informational texts as they practiced in the classroom library. He was not surprised by the success his students experienced in using informational texts or the excitement they displayed in reading these books.

DANNY PLAYS AT READING AN INFORMATIONAL TEXT

Let's look at Danny as he reads in the classroom library and utilizes his new-found skills in coming to understand how informational texts work. Today Danny has selected a book from the "Ocean Animals" container. He can't wait to see what the book holds, so he

[1]For additional information about text features, see *Text Forms and Features: A Resource for Intentional Teaching* (Mooney 2001).

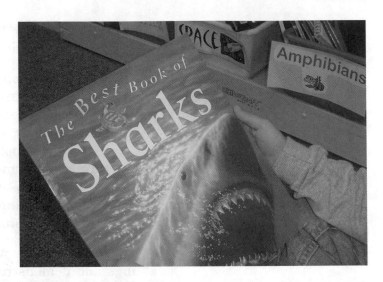

Figure 5.1: The cover of *The Best Book of Sharks*

starts right in, reading the book to a reading buddy. As you read keep in mind that what Danny reads is written in bold and what he says or does during his reading is written in italics. The notes explain the significance of what Danny is doing as he reads.[2]

Sharks! Danny exclaims.

Notes: Danny knows where the front of the book is. He also understands that the front of the book holds the title. When asked to point to the title of this book after he read it, Danny pointed to the largest word on the cover, "Sharks." Danny has some knowledge of sound/letter correspondence and identified the "s" when asked how he knew that was the word "sharks." When asked about the words that were above "Sharks," he said he didn't know them except, "I know that word. It's the word 'the'." Danny is making meaning from the pictures, using what he knows about sound/letter correspondence, and letting go of what he does not yet understand.

[2]All images from the book *The Best Book of Sharks* (Llewellyn 2005) are used by permission of the publisher.

Figure 5.2: The title page

Sharks! he says again, with the same enthusiasm.

Notes: Even though there is a different illustration on the title page, Danny doesn't change the title he has given the book. He understands that a title is a title and it remains the same from the cover to the title page.

Figure 5.3: The table of contents

With a serious look on his face, Danny scans the pictures on the table of contents—quickly turning the page and saying nothing.

Notes: The format of a table of contents is a new idea for Danny. When asked after he read what these pages are for, Danny shrugged his shoulders. This indicates that Danny's teacher needs to articulate to students how informational texts are structured. He will demonstrate to the class that they can locate specific information by using the table of contents.

Figure 5.4: Pages 4 and 5

Danny looks at page 4 and says, **Sharks have long teeth—long teeth.**

His eyes stare at the picture on page 5 and he says, **Sharks have big, long fins.**

Notes: Danny's eyes immediately go to the illustration on the right-hand page, but he goes back to the left-hand page as he reads. By reading the page that contains the text, he is beginning to understand that print holds meaning. Danny is a bit tentative about reading this new book, but it is obvious right from the start that he has some understanding of the structure of informational text.

Figure 5.5: Pages 6 and 7

He turns to pages 6 and 7. ***Sharks eat all kinds of fish.*** Danny notices a big, spotted shark at the bottom of the right-hand page and reads, ***Sharks sometimes eat tiger fish.*** He also notices a hammerhead shark and continues reading, ***Sharks even have two long eyes.***

Notes: Just as with his narrative reading, Danny attends to the detail in the pictures closely. He is using the detail to support his reading of this expository text. He understands that early informational texts often have sentence structures that are similar to each other. During this reading Danny begins each sentence with the word "sharks," but he shifts the next word in each sentence to give some intonation to his reading.

Figure 5.6: Pages 8 and 9

Sharks have big, long tails—and long fins.

Notes: This book is more complicated than Danny is used to. He is attending to the illustration on the bottom of page 9 but adds on to his reading after noticing the labeled diagrams at the top of the page.

Figure 5.7: Pages 10
and 11

Danny focuses on the large illustration on page 10 and says, ***Fish have big, long, skinny tails.*** He looks to the right and says, ***Other sharks have big, long tails.***

Figure 5.8: Pages 12
and 13

Notes: Danny only attends to the illustrations from which he can make meaning. The illustrations that he can't identify or make sense of he ignores and seems content with the results.

Danny smiles as he reads, **Sharks have two long eyes.** He studies the "feeding frenzy" on page 13 for a short while and then turns the page in anticipation.

Figure 5.9: Pages 14 and 15

Sharks even . . . Danny stops and looks puzzled for a moment. He searches the pictures on pages 14 and 15 and tries to correct himself. He studies the pictures on the right-hand side of the book and reads **Worms have big, sharp teeth, too.** Danny still isn't happy. He returns to the illustration on the left and continues **Sharks have bigger teeth than worms.** He looks at the right-hand page again and reads **Turtles swim slow.** Satisfied, he turns the page.

Notes: Danny struggles with all the different illustrations on this page. On his initial reading attempt, "Worms have big, sharp teeth," he returns to the familiar structure of narrative text by describing what is in the picture. He continues to look at the illustrations and realizes that what he said doesn't fit with the topic of the book. After a brief pause, he makes a correction by comparing the worm's teeth to those of sharks. The fact that Danny knew what he said had to somehow relate to sharks shows how he is further developing his understanding of expository texts.

Figure 5.10: Pages 16 and 17

Sharks eat people. Sharks eat spiders. Sharks eat wood. Sharks eat fish.

Notes: Notice how Danny continues with the same sentence structure for his reading of pages 16 and 17. With fewer illustrations to attend to, Danny seems to have an easier time focusing and reads with greater ease.

Figure 5.11: Pages 18 and 19

On page 18, Danny continues, **Sharks . . . Sharks hide underground so they can keep the fish and eat them up. Fish don't know they're there so they won't step away from there.**

Notes: Danny applies the content knowledge that he has been learning in science—how animals protect themselves with camouflage.

After finishing the publishing of the other students' writing, as he did with Danny earlier, the teacher calls all the students from their centers for a whole group lesson at the rug. Danny leaves the classroom library to take the book to his cubby. He knows that he can keep the book and finish his research later. The teacher asks if he needs a bookmark so he won't lose his place. Danny smiles and grabs one from the can where the homemade bookmarks are kept. He inserts the bookmark into the book, takes it to his cubby, and makes his way to the rug.

MONITORING DANNY'S INFORMATIONAL READING

Danny has improved immensely in his understanding of informational text over the past few weeks. His teacher regularly monitors the practice of his students in the classroom library. At this point in time Danny's teacher is monitoring his students' use of informational text. His teacher will maintain that focus for a few weeks in order to record notes on all of his students. He makes notes as to those elements of informational text his students control and those elements that need more work. Figure 5.12 contains an example of his monitoring notes.

Whether it's using narrative or informational text, playing at reading expands a student's oral language, attention to detail, and book-handling skills the more it is practiced.

Whether it's using narrative or informational text, playing at reading expands a student's oral language, attention to detail, and book-handling skills the more it is practiced. Incorporating playing at reading, whether in the classroom library or through reading instruction, answers a number of questions that early primary teachers have been asking about comprehension for a long time: What does explicit comprehension instruction look like in early primary classrooms? How might young students who have a specific learning need regarding comprehension be grouped and instructed? Chapter 6 responds to these questions and more by showing how a teacher uses a wordless book with a small group of first-grade students who are already reading but have been overfocused on reading the words rather than on comprehending the text.

Name: *Danny*   Date: *1/17*
Center: *Classroom Library*

Activity: *assessment—The Best Book of Sharks*
Last Assessed: *10/22—Narrative Text*

Notes

Strengths: *Used <u>Sharks</u> as title, understands title page contains title, carefully searched the pictures; handled the book confidently to tell a consistent story; started talking about worms on page 14/15 but quickly got back to shark topic; used description; Used some key vocabulary—fins, sharp teeth; used basic sentence structure of informational text—began many sentences with Sharks...*

Next Steps: *How to use Table of Contents; needs to understand that many pictures on a page have commonalities—sticking to the topic; attend to more of the print within the text*

Figure 5.12: The teacher's monitoring notes on Danny

Chapter 6 Small Group Reading Instruction

Stories have yet another magical quality: fully developed sentences borrowed from someone else. The dialogue can change a child from inarticulate embarrassment to confidence, as if by a magic wand. The only task required is to memorize the words. With enough practice, anyone can do this, because practice is part of the reward.

Vivian Gussin Paley (1981, 122)

In this first-grade classroom, the teacher has gathered four students at her table for reading instruction. These children are some of the more experienced or proficient readers and writers in class, but the teacher has noticed that when they are in the classroom library they look for only easy reading books to read during library time. Since these students have many skills in reading and writing at the letter and word level, which include control of sound-to-letter correspondence at the beginning, middle, and end of words, one-to-one matching, return sweep, and a growing sight vocabulary, they are excited when they can find books that match these skills. For that reason, the teacher has leveled book boxes for them to choose from in order to extend their reading skills on a daily basis. The leveled book boxes are for the independent practice of reading.

The classroom library in this classroom, however, serves a different purpose. A majority of the books in the classroom library are intentionally beyond many students' reading abilities. This first-grade teacher wants her students to use the classroom library to explore books, but more specifically to use pictures to tell stories from these more difficult texts. She wants them to practice telling a story in order to continue to develop their comprehension skills as well as increasing their knowledge of how narrative and expository texts work. From her demonstrations of using pictures in both narrative and expository texts to gain more meaning, many of her students have become quite skillful at comprehending more difficult texts. The four students selected for this group need to understand that there is more to reading than just reading the words. Their teacher wants them to read beyond the words. Paying closer attention to the pictures in stories will help them pull more meaning out of the books they read. This deeper meaning will support the development of reading skills that are usually reserved for more advanced readers—the elements of narrative and expository texts.

The support the teacher has chosen for this group is a wordless book about a boy and his dog. Using a wordless book allows the children to focus on the development of a story rather than just focusing on the literal level of the story—the words. The teacher's objective for the group is for them to tell a story using just the pictures. Because this is their first experience with a wordless book, the teacher anticipates that it will be a challenge for them not to have the words to rely on.

Each child will have a copy of the book and an opportunity to discuss what they read. Having used this book in prior years with children, the teacher knows that after reading the first few pages the children become comfortable and enjoy this type of reading. The teacher wants this reading group to look like any other reading group in which the students are reading silently. Let's look at how this first-grade teacher works with this small group of children and how she tries to meet her objective of using pictures to tell the story. As in previous chapters in this book, this chapter contains notes about the instruction that is occurring. As you read through the teacher/student interactions, take special interest in the notes that explain the teacher's intentions at critical points during that reading session.[1]

TEACHING COMPREHENSION IN A SMALL GROUP

Figure 6.1: Individual copies of *Best Friends*

Teacher: I've got a different kind of book today. Before I tell you why it's a different kind of book, who can tell me the name of this book?

All Students: *Best Friends*.

[1]All images from the book *Best Friends* (Cox 1999) are used by permission of the publisher.

Teacher: Why do you think it's called *Best Friends?* What might it be about?

All Students: Dogs.

Teacher: Just dogs?

Hanway: It's about a dog and a boy.

Christa: I think they're friends.

Nick: Me, too.

Teacher: Why do you think they're friends?

Christa: He's hugging the dog.

Hanway: I have a dog.

Teacher: It does look like the boy loves this dog. I bet you love your dog! (Hanway nods his head yes.)

Teacher: Do you think they're best friends?

All Students: Yes.

Christa: Jessica's my best friend.

Teacher: Oh, that's wonderful! Don't best friends have lots of fun together? Let's read and find out what this little boy and dog do because they're best friends. Now before we start, I told you this book is a little bit different—there are no words in this book. So if there aren't any words, how are we going to be reading it?

Hanway: The pictures?

Nick: Like in the library?

Teacher: That's right, just like reading in the library. We are going to read the pictures. You will be looking at pictures and thinking about the story. Let's make some more predictions about what we

Figure 6.2: The back cover

will read in the book. Turn over your book and let's look at the back cover. Let's see if the back cover tells us any more about the book.

Teacher: What do you notice about the picture on the back?

Hanway: There's another dog. One is yellow. The other one is black.

Christa: Maybe he has two dogs?

Teacher: Oh, I wonder if he has two dogs. That's a good "I wonder." Be thinking about that as we read this book. Let's start reading. Turn to the title page. What's the name of this book? Josh, will you read the name of the book for us?

Notes: As the teacher plans all aspects of her reading groups—before, during, and after—she thinks about the message or theme of the book. She does this because she wants her students to gain a deeper understanding of the story. The teacher decides the theme of *Best*

Friends is friendship; in particular "keeping old friends and making new ones." The teacher understands that the introduction to any book is a critical aspect in a reading group. It sets the stage for the thinking that students need as they approach a book. In planning the "before" part of the reading group or the introduction, the teacher wants to get her students thinking about the theme. She doesn't tell them the theme, but leads them to discover the theme as they make their way through the story. The teacher uses the clues given by the author and illustrator. In this introduction the teacher used the title, the picture on the front cover, and the students' background knowledge of friendship to begin the discussion. In an effort to spur further discussion and questions about what will happen within the book, the teacher also used the back cover, which shows the boy with another dog. This beginning discussion is setting the stage for her students to develop a deeper understanding of the story, *Best Friends*.

Figure 6.3: The title page

Josh: (Pointing to the words in the title and reading) ***Best Friends.***

Teacher: That's right—it's called *Best Friends* and it's by author Rhonda Cox. Let's find out about these best friends. Turn to the first two pages and read in your head to find out what these friends do. (All students look quietly at the pictures for a few moments.)

What did you find out? What do these best friends do with each other? Who would like to read for us? (All students look a bit perplexed).

What if I start off reading our story today? I think I'll call the boy Sam. He should have a name because he is an important character in our story.

Figure 6.4: Pages 2 and 3

Teacher: **Sam loves his dog . . . Peaches. Sam and Peaches do everything together. They like to spend time with each other. Their favorite thing to do is to go fishing. Sam puts the worm on the hook and holds the pole while Peaches stands guard, watching and waiting for the fish to come.**

That was fun! How was that reading? Did my story go along with the pictures? Would you like to try this?

All Students: Yes.

Nick: That's like me and my dog.

Teacher: That's great! Let's turn the page to see what else these two best friends do. Read in your head to find out.

Notes: As expected, the students are having a difficult time with this wordless book. This is why the teacher decided that the students would read the first two pages and then stop. She didn't want this group to get too far into the story if they weren't certain about what they were to do. The teacher was aware that she would need to model how to read a wordless book and that it would need to occur early in the book. When a teacher plans the "during" part of a reading group he or she needs to decide on good stopping points. These stopping points are places in the story where potential problems may occur or where there may be opportunities for discussion that leads to the development of the theme.

All students look quietly at the pictures for a few moments, then begin laughing and pointing to the dog wearing headphones at the top of page 4.

Figure 6.5: Pages 4 and 5

Teacher: What's so funny?

Nick: The dog is listening to music!

Hanway: He has headphones on! Dogs don't listen to music!

Teacher: All right, all right—who would like to read? Josh, why don't you read about this?

Josh: **The boy puts the headphones on the dog.**

Teacher: What else do Sam and Peaches do together? Keep reading.

Josh: **Sam and Peaches play in the woods.**

Nick: I think they love each other a lot and do everything together.

Teacher: I think so too. Let's keep reading. I wonder what else Sam and Peaches do. Read in your head (they turn to pages 6 and 7).

Figure 6.6: Pages 6 and 7

Teacher: What did you notice, Christa?

Christa: Sam is all by his-self.

Teacher: What do you think happened to Peaches? Christa, why don't you read for us?

Christa: **The boy is sad because he lost his dog.**

Hanway: I think he is going to look for him.

Teacher: What do you think Sam will do without his best friend Peaches?

Nick: I don't think he will have any fun because he is all alone.

Teacher: **All of a sudden Sam is by himself.** Where do you think Peaches is? Do you think there's a problem?

Josh: Yes. Peaches ran away.

Teacher: I'm wondering where Peaches is. I'm wondering what the problem is. Let's read the next few pages in our heads. Maybe we will find out what happened to Peaches.

Figure 6.7: Pages 8 and 9

The students start right in discussing the story on pages 8 and 9.

Hanway: They got lost. I think they got split up.

Teacher: Is that the problem? They got lost? Do we know for sure?

Josh: No.

Teacher: Hmmm, I wonder . . . Let's turn the page and read to find out.

Notes: Like all good stories, *Best Friends* has many of the elements of a narrative text. It has a beginning, a middle, and an ending, characters, a setting, an action, problem, or significant event, and a theme. When the reader puts a story to the pictures it would also be easy for them to use description, dialogue, and sensory detail. The teacher uses her knowledge of these elements and her knowledge of the reading process to engage her students. At this stopping point in the story the teacher uses anticipation of the problem to drive her students on in their reading. Thinking about the theme that she has identified (keeping old friends and making new ones), the teacher knows that she can use these stopping points to help build the students' understanding of the theme.

Figure 6.8: Pages 10 and 11

All Students (smiling at the pictures on pages 10 and 11): She had puppies!

Teacher: Oh, that was the problem. Peaches had puppies!

Nick: **Peaches went away to have her babies.**

Josh: Dogs like to be by themselves when they have babies.

Teacher: How are Peaches and Sam feeling now?

Nick: Good. He likes the puppies!

Teacher: Christa, what are you thinking?

Christa: Peaches went away to have her babies.

Teacher: What do you think is going to happen next? What is going to happen at the end of our story? Before you do read further, remember the back cover. (All students turn to the back cover.)

Josh: It's one of the puppies. He is going to keep one of the puppies.

Nick: Me, too.

Teacher: Do you all think so? (All students nod their heads yes.) Let's read the next four pages to find out. (The students go on to pages 12 through 15.)

Notes: To support the group's deeper understanding of the story, the teacher reminds the children of the question discussed in the introduction—why were there two different dogs on the front and back covers? The teacher knows that at this point in the story returning to those pictures will prompt more accurate predictions as the story draws to a close. She understands that she needs to support her students in making more accurate predictions that will help them get to a deeper meaning of the story.

Figure 6.9: Pages 12 and 13

Figure 6.10: Pages 14 and 15

Josh (reading across pages 12 through 15): **Sam plays with the puppies all the time, but he's sad. He doesn't want to give away the puppies.**

Hanway: You have to sell them when they're big enough.

Christa: He's not going to sell all of them. He keeps the black one.

Teacher: Sam is really holding on tight to that black puppy, isn't he? Is that how the story ends—Sam keeps one of the puppies? Let's read the last few pages and see.

Figure 6.11: Page 16 and the inside back cover

Teacher: So were we right? (All students nod their heads yes.) What happens?

Hanway: **The puppy gets in trouble all the time. He eats the shoes.**

Nick: My dog used to eat my shoes when he was a puppy.

Teacher: Yes, puppies do get in trouble. What should we call this puppy? I think he's another important character in our story. Let's give him a name.

Nick: Let's call him Blackie.

Hanway: Yeah, Blackie.

Teacher: All right! At the end of our story Sam gets to keep Blackie. So do you think that's why there's a black dog on the back cover? (turns to the back cover)

Hanway: Hey, that's the same picture that's on this page (turns to page 16 and points to the last picture).

Teacher: (smiling) Yes. It looks like it could be the same picture. What a great story! Who wants to tell us their ending?

Christa: I do! **Sam and Peaches will always be best friends.**

Josh: That's mine, too!

Nick: Mine is, **Sam and Blackie have lots of fun together and Peaches was happy to have one of her babies around so she wouldn't be lonely any more.**

Teacher: Those are great endings. Here's my ending—**Just because Sam has a new puppy doesn't mean he won't love**

Peaches. Having old friends is just as important as having new friends.

Notes: By the end of the story the students have a better idea of how to read a wordless book. As the teacher prompts the students to tell the ending of the story, she listens to the students' different versions and gains insight into the meaning that the students made during the instruction. While it is obvious that the students have varying degrees of understanding of the theme of *Best Friends,* the teacher offers her own version. Modeling a more in-depth ending reflecting a well-developed theme is another support for her students as they develop their comprehension skills.

USING WORDLESS BOOKS

By the time students reach third grade, many of their teachers complain that their students have trouble comprehending their reading. These teachers go on to say that their students can read the words or comprehend at literal levels but experience trouble thinking at higher levels of comprehension. Where does this trouble start? Does it start as soon as children enter third grade, or does it start sooner? In this first-grade classroom the teacher is monitoring the students' ability to comprehend beyond the written word. She understands that if young students spend all of their time reading just the words, especially at lower reading levels, they may miss the deeper meaning of stories. Much of the meaning of easy-to-read books is usually contained in the pictures. The teacher knows that young children need to understand the reading is about *making meaning,* not just reading words. The list in Figure 6.12 contains some of our favorite wordless or semi-wordless books, old and new, which teachers may want to use in developing the comprehension skills of their primary students.

The teacher knows that young children need to understand the reading is about *making meaning,* not just reading words.

Title	Author	Year	Publisher
Anno's Counting Book	Mitsumasa Anno	1975 (original)	Little Celebrations (Pearson) (current)
Best Friends	Rhonda Cox	1999	Richard C. Owen Publishers, Inc.
A Boy, a Dog, a Frog, and a Friend	Mercer and Marianna Mayer	1969-1975	Puffin Books
Car Trip	Donald Crews	1997	Celebration Press
Deep in the Forest	Brinton Turkle	1976	Dutton Books
The Flower Man	Mark Ludy	2005	Green Pastures
Follow the String	Susan James	1997	Celebration Press
Frog Goes to Dinner	Mercer Mayer	1974	Puffin Books/Dial
Frog on His Own	Mercer Mayer	1973	Puffin Books/Dial
Frog, Where Are You?	Mercer Mayer	1969	Puffin Books
Good Dog, Carl	Alexandra Day	1985	Simon & Schuster
Hug	Jez Alborough	2000	Candlewick Press
Little Turtle	Valerie Sommerville	2001	Richard C. Owen Publishers, Inc.
The Mitten	Andy San Diego	1997	Celebration Press
Noggin and Bobbin in the Snow	Oliver Dunrea	1997	Celebration Press
One Frog Too Many	Mercer and Marianna Mayer	1975	Dial
Oops	Pat Cummings	1997	Celebration Press
Pancakes for Breakfast	Tomie DePaola	1978	Harcourt Brace
The Pumpkin	Little Celebrations Series	1999	Celebration Press
The Red Book	Barbara Lehman	2004	Houghton Mifflin
School	Emily Arnold McCully	1987	HarperCollins
Tabby: A Story in Pictures	Aliki	1995	HarperCollins
Tuesday	David Weisner	1992	Houghton Mifflin
What's That Noise?	William Carman	2002	Random House
The Wind	Monique Felix	1991	Creative Editions

Figure 6.12: Recommended wordless and semi-wordless books

Developing comprehension skills are also reinforced by teaching that closely links reading and writing. Because there is a strong connection between reading and writing, writing can also be used to expand a student's understanding of oral language, attention to detail, and book-handling skills. With this in mind, the closer the instruction between reading and writing in early primary classrooms, the stronger a foundation the young children will develop. Chapter 7 explores beginning writing instruction and its connection in reinforcing how books and stories work.

Chapter 7   The Interrelatedness of Reading and Writing

Writing is a personal activity in which we compose messages which we put down to be read. The writing part of any early literacy intervention is not done just as a service to learning to read; it is not merely an activity engaged in to prepare a child to be a reader. In the end students should move forward with relative independence into any of the writing tasks demanded by the educational system. And reading and writing activities should continue to enrich each other.

Marie Clay (2001, 28)

When confronted with a challenge, readers break words down into smaller units (letters and/or letter chunks) in an effort to more fully understand what they are reading. This process is referred to as *decoding* (National Institute of Child Health and Human Development 2000, 10). When we write we build up—moving from smaller parts to larger parts or from letters to words to sentences. The more proficient we are in our ability to "build up" the more we are able to get across our message to readers. This process is known as *encoding*. Decoding and encoding letters, sounds, words, and sentences are reciprocal processes in reading and writing. When students apply what they know from reading to writing, teachers get a much clearer picture of what students understand about those literacy skills and what they don't know.

CHARACTERISTICS OF EMERGENT WRITERS

Oral language and attending to picture detail are reciprocal processes that should be used in both early reading and writing instruction.

Like decoding and encoding, understandings about written language (how books work and how stories work) apply to both reading and writing. Oral language and attending to picture detail are reciprocal processes that should be used in both beginning reading and writing instruction. As you look at the following list of characteristics of emergent writers, compare them to the characteristics of emergent readers listed in Chapter 1. Note the similarities between the two sets of characteristics and how they relate to the development of oral language and attention to detail. For example, in the "Behaviors as Readers" section in Chapter 1, one of the characteristics is "Uses pictures to predict text." In the "Behaviors as Writers" section below there is a comparable characteristic, "Draws pictures and scribbles to generate and express ideas." This particular example highlights the strong connection between the characteristics of emergent readers and writers. A young reader/writer cannot "use pictures" in reading or "draw pictures" in writing without using or noticing details. Furthermore, both sets of characteristics support oral language, as evidenced by the use of the words "predict" and "express." Almost all of the characteristics of emergent readers and writers have strong connections to oral language and attention to picture detail.

Attitudes toward Writing
- Is eager to play at writing
- Has confidence that personal experience is expressed with meaning in own writing

- Is encouraged by own success to write again
- Expects writing to be enjoyable
- Finds writing rewarding
- Expects own writing to belong to self.

Understandings about Writing

- Print holds meaning
- Stories can be written down
- Speech can be written down
- Writing can be read over and over again
- Begins to understand that thoughts can be written down
- Is responsible for own topics and learning
- Is developing an understanding of how books and stories work
- Is learning to write by watching the teacher's models and from own knowledge of familiar texts
- Expects the teacher to help in developing text
- Begins to realize that words are always spelled the same.

Behaviors as Writers

- Orients a page to start writing
- Develops some knowledge of directionality, spaces between words, upper- and lowercase letters
- Uses own experiences for writing
- Is beginning to locate references, such as students' names
- Centers topics largely on own world
- Draws pictures and scribbles to generate and express ideas
- Explains orally about own pictures
- Is able to make corrections when text is read back by the teacher
- Asks questions about others' stories
- Adds on to own story

- Experiments with letter shapes to arrive at consistency of letter form
- Uses pictures as a basis for writing
- Is prepared to attempt the spelling of unknown words by taking risks
- Shows some knowledge of alphabet through production of letter forms to represent message; develops sound/letter relationships
- Can recognize a few key words
- Has control of some essential words (adapted from Ministry of Education 1992, 121-124).

A TEACHING EPISODE WITH AN EMERGENT WRITER

The teacher in the following teaching episode is working to align her writing instruction with her reading instruction. As in her reading instruction, she knows that oral language and attending to picture detail need to be important aspects of her writing instruction as well.

Figure 7.1: The cover of *My Pictures and Stories* student booklet

In her classroom, the teacher has been working with the students using *My Pictures and Stories* (Matteson 2005), a writing book that supports students in telling stories through drawing pictures and provides a record of each student's writing growth over time. Each student in her classroom has a *My Pictures and Stories* book and makes weekly entries in it.

Prior to the following writing conference based upon the picture Kaylee drew in her *My Pictures and Stories* book, the teacher asked Kaylee about her weekend. Kaylee told the teacher about how she had hurt her foot on Saturday. Kaylee used her writing book to draw the picture of what happened when she hurt her foot. When she finished drawing her picture, shown in Figure 7.2, the teacher talked

Figure 7.2: Kaylee's original picture and story about hurting her foot

with her about it. Notice as she interacts with Kaylee how the teacher focuses on developing Kaylee's oral language and attention to picture detail. Think about how this writing experience is much like the playing at reading experiences discussed earlier in this book. The notes within this chapter help explain the significance of the teacher's interactions with Kaylee, both as a writer and as a reader.

Teacher: Tell me about your picture.

Kaylee: This is me and this is the doctor (pointing to the figures).

Teacher: Well, tell me what happened first. Why were you with your doctor?

Kaylee: 'Cause I bumped my foot at the playground with Mommy.

Teacher: Oh, you were at the playground and hurt your foot? What are these lines for? (pointing to the lines around Kaylee's head in the drawing)

Kaylee: I was crying.

Teacher: Were you smiling (pointing to the smile in the picture) when you were crying? (Kaylee quickly picks up a brown crayon and changes the smile to a frown.)

Teacher: What were you saying when you were crying?

Kaylee: I was saying, "Mom, Mom, I hurt my foot!"

Teacher: Is that what this says in your writing? (Kaylee nods her head. Teacher writes "Mom, Mom, I hurt my foot!" on a self-stick note to help her remember Kaylee's story when she comes back to it at a later date.)

When a student draws a picture and has a story to tell, the teacher needs to record the student's message so she can help the student remember the story over time.

Notes: When a student draws a picture and has a story to tell, the teacher needs to record the student's message so she can help the student remember the story over time. This teacher understands that recording a student's message can help her to support Kaylee in meeting many of the characteristics of emergent writers, especially in the area of emergent understandings of writing—print holds meaning, stories can be written down, speech can be written down, writing can be read over and over again, and that thoughts can be written down. When working with a student who has the skills that Kaylee exhibits, it might be preferable to record the message on another piece of paper such as a self-stick note and affix it to the back of the drawing so as not to interfere with the self-confidence of a beginning writer.

Teacher: I wonder what we could put in the picture to show that you hurt your foot. (Kaylee thinks for a moment and then picks up the brown crayon again and draws some lines around her sore foot.)

Teacher: What are those lines for?

Kaylee: That's my hurt foot.

Teacher: Wow! That looks like it hurt a lot! What happened at the end of your story?

Kaylee: Mommy took me to the doctor's.

Teacher: So you went to the playground and bumped your foot. It hurt so badly that you cried. Then Mom took you to the doctor's. (Kaylee nods her head.) What a great story to tell the other kids! Do you think they will want to hear your story about going to the playground and bumping your foot?

Kaylee: Yes.

Teacher: I do, too. Will you tell it at sharing today?

Kaylee: (Nods her head) Can I tell the part about going to the doctor's?

Teacher: Yes, but save that part for last because it didn't happen until the end of your story—okay? (Kaylee nods her head again, jumps off her chair, and joins her friends.)

Notes: The teacher knows that an understanding of narrative elements not only helps students as they read, but also as they write. In Kaylee's story the teacher works with her to develop the beginning and ending of her story, the description of the character (herself)—crying versus smiling, and sensory detail—pain radiating from her foot.

Just before sharing time Kaylee showed the teacher another picture that she drew (independently) at the writing center, shown in Figure 7.3. The teacher smiled when she saw the picture and held the following conversation with Kaylee:

Figure 7.3: Kaylee's picture of the ending to her story

Teacher: What's this?

Kaylee: This is me getting a lollipop at the doctor's.

Teacher: Why did you get a lollipop?

Kaylee: Because he said I was all better.

Teacher: Wow, what a great ending to your story! I see the lollipop. Let's write the ending, "You're all better now, Kaylee." (Teacher writes the ending on a self-stick note) Now I think you are really ready to share your story with your friends.

Notes: Because the teacher's writing instruction is also influenced by the characteristics of emergent writers, it is easy to see how it results in this student's attitude about writing. Kaylee left her writing conference excited by her story. She knows that writing is about communicating and that it might need to be clarified. She knows that she is capable of conveying her message without help. In looking at the attitudes of emergent writers it is easy to see that Kaylee is eager to play at writing, has confidence that personal experience is expressed with meaning in her own writing, is encouraged by her own success to write again, expects writing to be enjoyable, finds writing rewarding, and expects her own writing to belong to herself.

TEACHING BASED ON STRONG UNDERSTANDINGS

In this teaching episode the teacher shows she understands that writing supports the same components found in reading. She understands that the elements of narrative text are as important in writing as they are in reading. This teacher made sure that her student was able to tell an important event with a strong structure—a good beginning, middle, and ending. She understands that a student's story needs to have a strong plotline—emphasizing the problem and solution. The teacher also understands that dialogue is an important component of a narrative—most stories have some dialogue, whether it is self-talk, thinking, or someone talking to someone else. She understands that students need to tell their stories to others and to get a listener's reaction to the story. How was the teacher able to accomplish all of this in one teaching episode? The teacher understands that in order to develop oral language there needs to be a structure that she can use to support the student. The teacher understands that narrative and expository elements provide a strong structure. She also understands that it's the detail in the picture, whether in reading or writing, that will support the telling and retelling of a narrative or expository text. The more opportunities children have to practice these structures, the more they come to incorporate them into everything they do in viewing, presenting, listening, speaking, reading, and writing.

How is this teacher able to keep her students moving along in their literacy development? How does she develop students who have a story to tell and want to articulate it like Kaylee? First and foremost, the teacher recognizes that both reading and writing are about telling a story. Emphasizing oral language and attention to picture detail through narrative elements in both reading and writing has created an atmosphere where Kaylee can easily see and make connections to what she was learning. Secondly, the teacher understands that it is important to continually assess her students. Monitoring growth in oral language and attention to picture detail is an essential component in Kaylee's literacy development. The teacher also understands that the assessment she uses needs to reflect the work her students do in class so she can record as accurate information as possible on each student.

First and foremost, the teacher recognizes that both reading and writing are about telling a story.

For these reasons this teacher uses the Early Literacy Continuum for Writing from *Assessing and Teaching Beginning Writers: Every Picture Tells a Story* (Matteson and Freeman 2005). The teacher understands that the Early Literacy Continuum for Writing will help her to support her students' ability to attend to the detail in pictures and to tell a well-developed story and thus support their literacy development. By aligning the child's drawing to the "Level of Student's Work" section of the continuum, the teacher can determine where the student is in relation to "attending to detail" and where she needs to go next. Similarly, by aligning the child's story about her picture to the "Level of Student's Oral Language" section of the continuum, the teacher can determine where the student is in relationship to her oral language development and make decisions about the next learning steps in her ability to tell a story. The middle section of the continuum, "Teaching Objectives," is where the teacher places her district's objectives, which she has lined up with the developmental levels of oral language and student work and uses as she works with students. The Early Literacy Continuum for Reading, presented in the next chapter of this book, is similar in structure to the writing continuum and involves a similar process of evaluating a student's oral language and his or her attention to detail.[1]

Think about the impact on the teaching and learning that will occur in a class when a teacher collects data, asks questions about it, and uses what she finds out to make appropriate instructional decisions. Think about the impact on teaching and learning when both reading and writing are monitored through very similar assessments. Like the Early Literacy Continuum for Writing, the Early Literacy Continuum for Reading measures a student's growth in oral language and attention to detail, but as it applies to playing at reading

Think about the impact on teaching and learning when both reading and writing are monitored through very similar assessments.

[1]For an in-depth look at how to use the Early Literacy Continuum for Writing, refer to *Assessing and Teaching Beginning Writers: Every Picture Tells a Story* (Matteson and Freeman 2005).

or book exploration. It is the use of these two continuums in prekindergarten and early primary classrooms that connects reading and writing and makes collecting data about a student's literacy development straightforward and manageable. Chapter 8 takes an in-depth look at the Early Literacy Continuum for Reading and its use in the classroom.

Chapter 8 Monitoring Reading Behavior

In order for formative assessment to be embedded in practice, it is vital that teachers have children's learning as their priority, not their teaching or the opinions of outside parties. This is easy to say, but less easy to implement.

Shirley Clark (2003, 2)

In order to be truly effective in teaching and in our ability to move students along in their literacy development, our classroom assessment and instruction must be closely related. The more instructional connections we can make for ourselves as teachers and for the students we teach, the more of an impact we have on the learning that occurs for our students. Chapter 7 looked at writing instruction and its connection to reading. In particular, it focused on how teachers can impact literacy through evaluating student work samples using the Early Literacy Continuum for Writing (Matteson and Freeman 2005). Chapter 8 takes an in-depth look at a reading continuum that similarly impacts literacy development. Like the Early Literacy Continuum for Writing, the Early Literacy Continuum for Reading focuses on a child's oral language development as well as his or her ability to attend to detail. The Early Literacy Continuum for Reading helps teachers evaluate these areas as it applies to the concept of playing at reading as emphasized in this book.

THE EARLY LITERACY CONTINUUM FOR READING

The Early Literacy Continuum for Reading is very similar to the Early Literacy Continuum for Writing discussed in Chapter 7. It, too, consists of three distinct sections. Just like the writing continuum, the two outer sections of the reading continuum focus on students' oral language and students' work. The Level of Oral Language sections are the most similar in both continuums. Just as in the writing continuum, the oral language section of the Early Literacy Continuum for Reading deals with a student's ability to tell a story. Both continuums contain oral language sections that consist of five boxes that represent five different developmental levels. These levels of oral language represent a range of ability for telling stories from not communicating and/or gesturing to listing words or using short phrases about individual pictures to telling a story that is complete, with many of the elements of narrative text.

The student's work section is where differences exist between the two continuums. The writing continuum focuses on the drawing of pictures as the basis for student work in writing, whereas the reading continuum focuses on book-handling skills or print concepts as the basis of student work in reading. The Levels of Book Handling Skills section of the reading continuum looks at a child's ability to handle books or at his or her understandings of print concepts. Like the writing continuum, this section of the reading continuum encompasses five different developmental levels. These levels of book-handling skills in the reading continuum range from randomly flipping

The reading continuum focuses on book-handling skills or print concepts as the basis of student work in reading.

Early Literacy Continuum for Reading

Levels of Book-Handling Skills	Teaching Objectives[1]	Levels of Oral Language[2] (in the language of instruction)
1. The student's interactions with books reveal very few understandings about print in place. The book may be upside down or backwards. The student randomly flips through the pages and will go through several books in a short period of time.	**Through individual pictures the student will be able to:** • Use pictures to tell a simple story • Use picture clues to infer and predict • Make connections between books/stories and their own experiences • Compare, predict actions, and draw conclusions through everyday experiences • Recognize patterns of sound (rhyming words).	1. The student will not converse about the book. However, he or she may point or gesture.
2. The student's interactions with books reveal more understanding about print. The book is held right side up, and the reader goes from front to back. The reading still involves flipping through the pages, but the reader will spend more time looking at the pictures. The student may go through several books in a short period of time.	**Through stories the student will be able to:** • Understand that pictures and print convey meaning • Tell a story with a beginning, middle, and ending • Develop phonemic awareness by listening to songs, nursery rhymes, dramatic activities, storytelling, and poetry • Recognize familiar letters or words found in his or her environment • Use new vocabulary in different contexts • Share a story with an audience • Select books, tapes, and music related to things they are interested in or are learning about • Select poetry, fiction, and nonfiction from a variety of literature • Respond to text with meaningful questions and thoughtful comments.	2. The student names objects using words, short phrases, or simple sentences about the book through teacher questioning. However, the student may seem unsure of the story and/or give different responses during continued reading.
3. Basic understandings about print are secure. The student's interactions with books are more deliberate. The pace of reading is slowed by the reader's attention to pictures. The student picks out detail, but it may be random and *not critical* to the story.		3. The student names objects using words, short phrases, or simple sentences about the book. The language and story remains constant during the reading and re-reading *over time*.
4. The student's interactions with books show attention to the detail critical to the story but may ignore any print on the page.		4. The student begins to tell a simple story about the book through teacher questioning.
5. The student's interactions with books show attention to detail critical to the story, and the student notices some print on the page.	**The student will be able to:** • Follow written text when text is read aloud • Recognize some letters and know some sound/symbol relationships.	5. The student is able to tell a story about the book with little or no teacher support.

© 2006 by Deborah K. Freeman and David M. Mattteson

[1]Objectives taken from Aurora Public Schools Preschool Continuum.
[2]In ELL/ESL and bilingual classrooms, the teacher evaluates the student's performance in the language of instruction. For example, in a Spanish bilingual classroom, the language of instruction is Spanish. In any ELL/ESL classroom, the language of instruction is English.

Figure 8.1: The Early Literacy Continuum for Reading as adapted by Aurora Public Schools

pages to paying more deliberate attention to pictures to focusing on aspects of pictures and words that are critical to the telling of a story.

The third section of the Early Literacy Continuum for Reading is where the teaching objectives can be found. This section is very similar to the Teaching Objectives section in the writing continuum. Like the writing continuum, the Teaching Objectives section of the reading continuum consists of three separate boxes in the middle of the continuum, where any district goals, state goals, and/or emergent characteristics can be placed. A school organizes their goals in one of the three boxes in the Teaching Objectives section. The goals that have a strong *conversational* component go into the first box. The goals that have a strong *print awareness* component go into the second box, and those goals that emphasize *print* go into the last box. The teacher uses these objectives to plan for teaching that responds to each child's developmental level in the Oral Language and Book-Handling Skills sections of the continuum. It could very well be that teachers will find many of the same objectives in both continuums. Both continuums have *strong* connections among all three sections—oral language, book-handling skills or student work, and teaching objectives. The lines that link the boxes within the continuum represent these connections. The reading continuum in Figure 8.1 was adapted by Aurora Public School's Early Childhood Program in Aurora, Colorado in order to align their beginning reading instruction to their beginning writing instruction. They adapted the Early Literacy Continuum for Writing in 2004 (Matteson and Freeman 2005). A generic reading continuum is shown in the appendix.

Unlike writing, reading seems more difficult to assess because there isn't a concrete product to evaluate. When Kaylee's teacher wanted to evaluate Kaylee's oral language and attention to detail in writing, she could assess her picture. The teacher could also assess Kaylee's oral language because the teacher talked with Kaylee about her picture and recorded her message. But how do we evaluate a young child's ability to play at reading? If attention to detail and telling a story are important beginning reading behaviors, what do we assess? What's the concrete evidence of a student's attention to detail and oral language development when it applies to reading? Let's look as a teacher uses the Early Literacy Continuum for Reading to assess one of her student's reading behaviors as he reads with her in the classroom library.

THE CONTINUUM IN ACTION

Sergio, a four year old, is in the classroom library. The teacher notices him flipping through several books, not attending to any particular aspects of the books. She has seen him do this on his many trips to the classroom library. The teacher decides to assess his beginning reading skills. She pulls a book off the bookshelf where she keeps picture books that she uses to assess what her students know about books and what they know about telling stories through using pictures. The books on this shelf contain clear but detailed pictures that carry strong story-lines or strong beginnings, middles, and endings. The settings and characters in these stories offer wonderful opportunities for students to use description and dialogue as they look at the pictures and tell the stories housed within them. These stories also contain familiar messages or themes that support a student's ability to tell the story. The book the teacher has chosen to assess Sergio is entitled *Kiss Good Night* by Amy Hest (2001). The theme of *Kiss Good Night* is nighttime fears. The teacher has used this book before with other students and feels that Sergio will relate to it easily. In short, the teacher thinks *Kiss Good Night* will present good opportunities for her to gain information

Figure 8.2: Assessment book used for Sergio

not only about Sergio's book-handling skills but also about his ability to tell a story. The following is the dialogue between Sergio and his teacher as she assesses his oral language and book-handling skills. There are notes throughout the dialogue explaining the teacher's thinking or actions during the assessment.

As Sergio's teacher approaches him in the classroom library, she sits next to him so that as the assessment is conducted they will both view the book from the same perspective. Without showing Sergio the book, the teacher starts the assessment by saying: *I've got this wonderful book that I want you to see. Do you think you can tell me the story that's in this book?* Sergio smiles and says nothing.

The teacher gives the book to Sergio with the spine facing him and says: *Before you start, can you show me the cover of the book?* Sergio takes the book and places the book on the table with the cover facing up, but upside down. He points to the front cover but leaves the book upside down.

The teacher waits a moment to see if Sergio will turn the book around, then asks: *Can you point to the title?* Sergio still says nothing, but points to the title, which is still upside down.

Notes: The teacher doesn't react too quickly to the book being upside down. She wants to see what Sergio will do. She decides to continue with the assessment without turning the book to see what will occur as he works with the book further.

The teacher asks: *What do think the book is called?*

Sergio says quietly, ***The Bears.***

The teacher continues: *What do you think the book is going to be about?*

Sergio says, *Bears.*

Because he gave so little information, the teacher asks: *Anything else?* Sergio says nothing.

The teacher says: *Open the book and show me where the story begins.* Sergio opens the book (still upside down) to the first page.

The teacher says: *Take a look at all the pictures in the book by yourself and think about the story.* Sergio flips through the first few pages (all upside down).

Notes: As Sergio is flipping through the pictures upside down, the teacher looks at the Early Literacy Reading Continuum to see where Sergio might be. At this point in the assessment the teacher thinks that Sergio is on Level 1 of the continuum's section on book-handling skills because he hasn't turned the book right side up. However, the teacher decides to continue to see what other book-handling skills he might exhibit. She does this because she knows that many times assessment situations do not reflect what normally happens when children are working independently.

After Sergio flips through the book the teacher turns the book around and says: *Go back to the beginning of the book and tell me the story you have in your head.* Sergio turns to the first page, which shows a nervous little bear looking out his window at a strong wind blowing leaves off a tree, and says nothing.

The teacher waits a moment to see if Sergio will use the picture to make a prediction about the story, then prompts: *Tell me about this picture.*

Sergio says quietly, ***The wind blow.***

Again the teacher waits to see what Sergio will do and then prompts: *Let's keep reading. Why don't you turn to the next page?* Sergio turns the page, looks at the picture of the mother bear putting the little bear to bed as the storm continues outside the window, and says nothing.

Again, the teacher prompts further: *Tell me about this picture.*

Sergio whispers, ***Shhhh.***

Sergio sits quietly. The teacher suggests: *Turn the page and keep telling the story.* The picture on this page shows the mother bear tightly tucking the little bear into his bed as he holds onto one of his stuffed animals. Sergio looks at the picture. He still says nothing.

The teacher waits a moment to see if Sergio will volunteer anything on his own, then she says:

Tell me about this picture.

Sergio says quietly, ***Nigh', nigh'***.

Notes: The teacher looks at the continuum again and sees that Sergio can attend to the pictures, but only with much prompting. Realizing that Sergio will need encouragement to talk about each picture, she decides that she will end the assessment. Before she ends, however, she wants to assess one more piece of information—what Sergio understands about the role of print. Although the emphasis of instruction indicated by the lower levels on the reading continuum is on talking about pictures and telling stories, the teacher wants to know early on what her students understand about print. The teacher understands that she can't wait until students reach those higher levels on the reading continuum to support them in that area.

To determine what Sergio knows about print, the teacher asks: *Where do you think it says **Nigh', nigh'**?* Sergio points to the picture of Mrs. Bear putting Sam to bed.

Again, Sergio sits quietly and does not turn the page. The teacher says: *You have worked really hard today. Why don't you take a break at the snack table?*

Notes: In reflecting on Sergio's assessment, the teacher thinks that Sergio has more skills than he is exhibiting. She is concerned that he kept the book upside down throughout most of their interaction. However, when she has seen him read in the classroom library the books he has been reading have usually been right side up. The teacher decides that because he did not correct the position of the book during the assessment that Sergio is on a Level 1 in his book-handling skills. She knows that this lower score may not represent what he usually does in reading, but she knows he needs to understand that books should be right side up *every* time he reads. She will teach him to always hold the book right side up when reading and will reassess him shortly.

In assessing his level of oral language or ability to tell a story, the teacher is also concerned that Sergio needed much prompting during the assessment. She has placed Sergio on Level 2 because she had to continually question or prompt him. This behavior on Sergio's part seems to indicate that he is unsure in his understanding that he can tell the story of the text through pictures. She would like to see him react more to the pictures and talk freely about what he is seeing in those pictures. The teacher thinks that having a reading partner may help him in that area. After the assessment the teacher fills out her monitoring notes on Sergio, as shown in Figure 8.3.

Name: *Sergio*   Date: *10/01*
Center: *Classroom Library*

Activity: *Assessment—Kiss Good Night*
Last Assessed: *N/A—New student*
Book Handling Score: *1*
Oral Language Score: *2*

Notes

Strengths: *Identified front of book and title; was able to talk about pictures with much prompting*

Next Steps: *Needs to keep book right side up; needs more opportunities to talk about pictures—pair him up to read with a partner; needs to start acknowledging print*

Figure 8.3: The monitoring notes from Sergio's playing at reading assessment

ASSESSING DIFFERENT LEVELS OF LEARNERS

Teacher monitoring and recording of beginning reading behavior is an important aspect in teaching. In an effort to develop these practices, monitoring and recording need to be easy to manage, easy to access, and easily understood by anyone. Sergio's assessment and monitoring notes are wonderful examples of how this teacher is working to meet these three assessment monitoring and recording criteria. Let's consider the vignettes of children playing at reading contained in Chapters 4 and 5 and what the recording of their beginning reading behavior could look like written down. Even though Danessa in Chapter 4 was not in a classroom, we can consider her oral language and book-handling skills as an example of how to score a child using the reading continuum. Danessa is an excellent example of a student who would score at Level 4 in her book-handling skills. She moved through the story page by page and paid attention to the details within the illustrations that helped her tell the story with meaning. To move her on in her development as a reader, Danessa's teacher needs to do more to support her in making a transition from the pictures to print. Danessa needs to attend to the print in both the title and the text more as she continues to play at reading.

In thinking about Danessa's oral language development as it relates to reading, her score would be at the highest level—Level 5. As she read, Danessa displayed good intonation, a memory for text, and problem-solving skills. Not only did Danessa's father allow her to read the book, he kept silent as she worked to recall some of the meaning of the text. Because Danessa is skillful at playing at reading, she was allowed to work through making meaning of the pictures. As we teach, we need to see if our teaching has been effective.

Building independence is an important aspect in developing a reader.

Building independence is an important aspect in developing a reader. The last level of the continuum is a level of independence for these beginning readers. A desirable outcome for children at this level would be for them to transfer this knowledge to other areas in the classroom or to other genres while continuing to practice reading. Because a student is proficient at playing at reading with one genre doesn't mean he or she will be proficient at another. An excellent next teaching point for Danessa would be to have her begin to work with expository texts. Monitoring notes for Danessa might look like the example in Figure 8.4.

Name: *Danessa*   Date: *10/01*
Center: *Classroom Library*

Activity: *Where's Arthur's Gerbil?*
Last Assessed: *n/a*
Book Handling Score: *4*
Oral Language Score: *5*

Notes

Strengths: *Very independent—moved through it page by page; told the story with meaning; displayed good intonation, a memory for text, and problem-solving skills*
Next Steps: *Begin work with expository texts*

Figure 8.4: Monitoring notes with assessment scores for Danessa

Let's look closely at Danny in Chapter 5 and how he would have scored on the continuum for reading had the teacher used his reading of *The Best Book of Sharks,* an expository text, as an assessment. Danny's book-handling skills definitely place him at Level 4 on the reading continuum. He spent time carefully looking over each page,

---

Name: *Danny*　　Date: *1/17*
Center: *Classroom Library*

Activity: *assessment—The Best Book of Sharks*
Last Assessed: *10/22—Narrative Text*
Book Handling Score: *4*
Oral Language Score: *2*

Notes

Strengths: *Used <u>Sharks</u> as title, understands title page contains title, carefully searched the pictures; handled the book confidently to tell a consistent story; started talking about worms on page 14/15 but quickly got back to shark topic; used description; Used some key vocabulary—fins, sharp teeth; used basic sentence structure of informational text—began many sentences with Sharks...*

Next Steps: *How to use Table of Contents; needs to understand that many pictures on a page have commonalities—sticking to the topic; attend to more of the print within the text*

Figure 8.5: Monitoring notes with assessment scores for Danny

indicating that he was searching the pictures. He handled the book confidently and worked at attending to the critical detail within the pictures to tell a consistent story. He was also attending to the print of the title. However, Danny also needs to be more consistent and attend to some of the print within the story. "Attending to more of the print within the story" would be his next learning step and support his advancement to Level 5 on the reading continuum.

In looking over his oral language development as it relates to reading expository texts, Danny would be at Level 2. At times Danny seemed unsure about how to handle this expository text, as evidenced by his switching between the elements of the expository and narrative genres. Many times a student's score may be lower as they work to understand and incorporate new genres into their reading ability. For Danny, a good teaching point would be to focus on the elements of expository texts, such as knowing how a Table of Contents page works or keeping to the topic. Danny's monitoring notes might look something like those in Figure 8.5 if *The Best Book of Sharks* was used as an assessment.

MAKING LEARNING DECISIONS

When the Early Literacy Continuum for Writing is used in conjunction with the Early Literacy Continuum for Reading, not only will teachers make stronger reading and writing connections for their students, they will also make better learning decisions as well. Aurora Public School's Early Childhood Education Program is working toward making better learning decisions for their youngest learners. For the past few years the program coordinators have been closely monitoring their students' oral language and attention to detail through use of the Early Literacy Continuum for Writing. Now they are collecting the same type of information through the Early Literacy Continuum for Reading. Chapter 9 looks at the reading data they have collected in their first year of using the Early Literacy Continuum for Reading.

Chapter 9   Collecting and Using the Data

> Assessment is the stance that allows us to learn from our students and thus to teach them. Assessment is the compass with which we find our bearings and chart our course, and the map on which we do this.
>
> Lucy McCormick Calkins (2001, 137)

Chapter 8 looked at how the Early Literacy Continuum for Reading helps teachers monitor beginning reading skills, in particular monitoring how students attend to the details in pictures and tell a story. Chapter 9 looks at how teachers can use the data from that monitoring to inform their instruction and how in turn districts can use the same information to set student achievement goals and/or set targets for professional development.

In Colorado in the past few years, the leadership team of Aurora Public School's (APS) Early Childhood Education Program has focused on their students' writing by using the Early Literacy Continuum for Writing (Matteson and Freeman 2005). In an effort to help them teach their beginning readers more effectively, the professional development focus for teachers has shifted to include the development of the reader as well as the writer. Understanding that writing and reading are closely linked and that consistency is very important, APS's Early Childhood Education Program has begun using the Early Literacy Continuum for Reading in conjunction with the Early Literacy Continuum for Writing. This chapter outlines how APS's Early Childhood Education Program is using information from the Early Literacy Continuum for Reading.

INTERPRETING THE READING DATA FOR CLASSROOM USE

In the following graphs we see the results from APS's Early Childhood Education Program's first quarterly (November) reading assessment using the Early Literacy Continuum for Reading. These graphs reflect their students' levels of oral language and attention to detail as it relates to reading. The first graph, in Figure 9.1, focuses on the oral language portion of the reading continuum. With the results graphed, teachers have insight into each student's ability to tell a story or oral language development. The last bar on this graph represents the average oral language level of the class. Using an average bar in a graph helps draw attention to certain information. For example, in this graph, six out of thirteen students are above the average range and five students are below the average of the class. Two students, new to the class, still need to be assessed. These new students are not included in the average.

Graphing student data makes the learning patterns of students more visible.

Graphing student data makes the learning patterns of students more visible. When teachers use graphs, they have opportunities to reflect on their students' performance. Some of the questions teachers ask themselves as they review their classroom graphs are:

- Who is making good progress? Why? How will I continue to help them progress?

- Who is not making the kind of progress I want? Why? What can I do to accelerate their progress?
- Who do I need to monitor more closely? How will I do that and what will I look for?
- Are there discrepancies between the levels of student work and oral language? If so, why, and what will I do about it?
- How does all this help me plan for instruction?

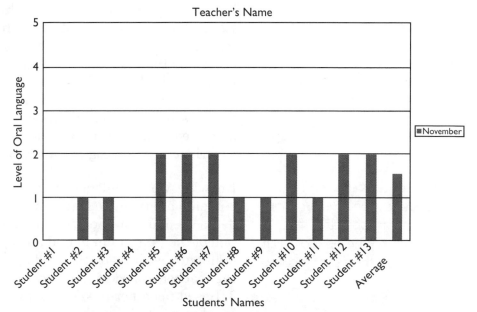

Figure 9.1: Classroom graph showing individual levels of oral language

Asking and answering questions like these has a significant impact on teachers' instruction and allows them to better consider the "who," "what," and "how" of daily and weekly planning for instruction. Let's look at how this graph helps a teacher in planning whole group, small group, and/or individual reading instruction.

The majority of students on this graph are on Level 2 of the oral language section on the reading continuum. This is useful information when planning for whole group reading instruction. Reading demonstrations are an effective way to introduce new skills to the whole class. In order to think about what these students as a whole need to know next, the teacher needs to think about the skills that were previously taught and what most have mastered. For example, the teacher of this class might feel confident that most of her students, especially those on Level 2, understand the school district's objectives from the first box on the reading continuum; that is they use pictures to tell a simple story, use picture clues to infer and predict, make connections between books/stories and their own experiences, compare and predict actions as well as draw conclusions through everyday experiences, and recognize patterns of sound (rhyming words).

The teacher uses the Teaching Objectives section of the continuum to find an objective that corresponds to the next oral language level on the reading continuum.

Knowing what students already know helps teachers identify what students are ready to learn. In order to plan for what most of her students need to know next, the teacher uses the Teaching Objectives section of the continuum to find an objective that corresponds to the next oral language level on the reading continuum. For this particular class the teacher looked at the teaching objectives that correspond to Level 3. Based upon her previous instruction and the information she analyzed from the November reading assessment, the teacher selects the objective, "Tell a story with a beginning, middle, and ending" as the next step for the whole group. Now during her reading demonstrations the teacher will emphasize the beginning, middle, and ending of stories. Knowing where students are instructionally and where they need to go next makes choosing an objective easier.

Using the same information from this graph, the teacher can also think about how to group her students for small group instruction as she works with them in the classroom library. Teachers can use the information to help them flexibly group their students—such as mixed ability grouping or grouping according to need. In looking at the data from this particular class, the large group of Level 2 students may need to be divided into two or three smaller groups. These smaller groups of two or three students often make teaching and learning more effective. Depending on how the teacher decides to group these students, her objectives may be different for each student or group.

From the information in the graph in Figure 9.1, the teacher might also decide that the students who scored at Level 1 need to meet with her more often than the others in order to spend more time working with a chosen objective in an attempt to accelerate their progress. Thinking about this group of students, the teacher knows that they understand how to "use pictures to tell a simple story," but only on individual pages. The teacher wants them to be able to carry the story over many pages, so she decides on the objective of "Using picture clues to infer and predict." She knows this objective will help these two students learn to tell a story using all the pictures within a book. No matter how a teacher decides to group students, using a variety of data to inform his or her decisions will make instruction more effective and efficient.

The next graph, from the same class, highlights the November assessment results as they relate to book-handling skills (Figure 9.2). Again, using the last bar of the graph (the average of the class), notice which students are above the average, which are below the average, and who needs to be assessed. The same reflective questions and instructional decisions that were made based on the oral language graph in Figure 9.1 also apply to this graph on book-handling skills.

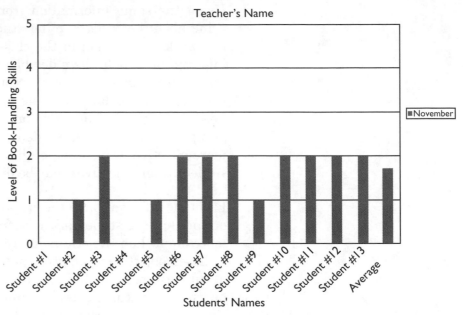

Figure 9.2: Classroom graph showing individual levels of book-handling skills

Useful information can also be gained by comparing the two graphs. Look at the average score of book-handling skills and compare it to the average score of oral language. You will see that the results are slightly higher for the students' book-handling skills than their oral language development. This is information that the teacher can use as she plans for instruction. This information should cause the teacher to ask:

- Am I creating enough opportunities for my students to talk?
- How can I create more opportunities?

INTERPRETING THE READING DATA FOR DISTRICT USE

The next two graphs were generated by the leadership team at APS's Early Childhood Education Program in order to determine trends across the district. The first graph (Figure 9.3) shows a total of all the district's four year olds' levels of oral language scores. The second graph (Figure 9.4) shows the total of scores for their book-handling skills levels. These graphs were created by totaling every student's score across the district using the results of November's assessment of the Early Literacy Continuum for Reading. All the Level 1s were

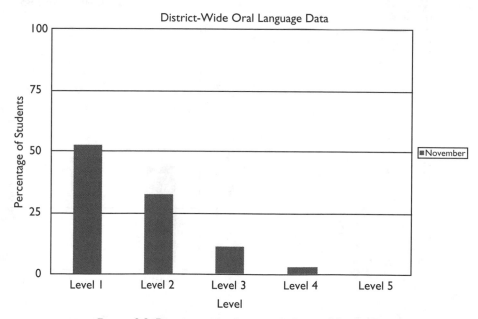

Figure 9.3: District-wide data graph for oral language

totaled together, as were the scores of Levels 2, 3, 4, and 5, to create a district-wide snapshot of their preschoolers.

The leadership team gained useful information when they compared the two graphs. For example, they noticed that the levels of book-handling skills were stronger overall for students than their levels of oral language skills. Questions arose about what this information might mean in terms of teacher and student strengths and learning needs. Many of the questions they asked were similar to the questions asked by teachers as they looked at their classroom data.

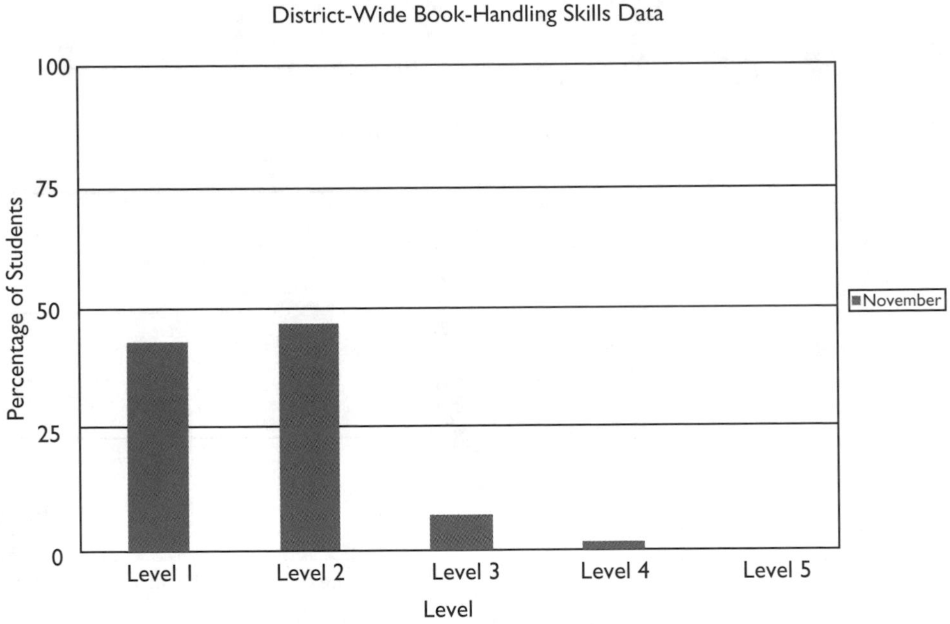

District-Wide Book-Handling Skills Data

Figure 9.4: District-wide data graph for book-handling skills

- Where are the majority of our students? Is that an appropriate level at this time of the year?
- Where do we want the majority of students to be by the next assessment? . . . by the end of the year? How do we get them there?
- Are there any discrepancies between the levels of student work and oral language? If so, why, and how will we help teachers bridge this gap?
- How does this information help us plan for teacher development?

As a result of their analysis of this data, subsequent conversations by the leadership team led to several possible professional development topics for teachers, such as:

- Increasing students' oral language skills
- Analyzing student work for instructional grouping
- Accelerating lower-performing students
- Meeting the needs of higher-performing students
- Best practices for emergent readers.

In developing other uses for these graphs, districts could use them to help set benchmarks for student progress throughout the year. By using the average bar in each graph, districts could set benchmarks for each area (Oral Language and Book-Handling Skills) as one way to inform teachers and parents as to how their students are doing compared to the "average" at a particular point in the year. Each year the average for each quarter is taken into account for the development of the benchmark for that quarter. This allows the district to create more "true" benchmarks—ones that are not set using a single year's averages. These benchmarks support teachers in making instructional decisions for each student's needs by asking:

By using the average bar in each graph, districts could set benchmarks for each area.

- What does the average student look like at this time of year?
- Which students are beyond the average and which ones are below the average? Why? And what do we need to do to help everyone progress or accelerate, as appropriate?

When districts use data of this nature to set goals and inform their decisions about inservice training, they have confidence that they are doing all that they can to provide teachers with the support they need to do their best job. Everyone benefits—districts benefit because students at all levels are being monitored as they move toward a common goal. Teachers benefit because they are provided with inservice training that meets their needs in the classroom. Students benefit because they receive instruction that is explicit, focused, and designed to meet their individual needs. The early literacy continuums, both for reading and for writing, are helping Aurora Public Schools' preschools do just that.

LEARNING BY DOING

As discussed in the opening paragraph of this chapter, APS's Early Childhood Education Program is using the Early Literacy Continuum for Reading to *develop* their teachers' and administrators' understandings of reading. That is exactly what the Early Literacy Continuum for Reading, as well as the Early Literacy Continuum for Writing, was designed to do: develop the knowledge of teachers and administrators who in turn would be able to more effectively develop the students with whom they work. These continuums were not meant to be thoroughly studied over a long period of time and then implemented. They were designed to be put to use right away as a support for the ongoing process of developing understandings about early literacy. They were designed to be a support for the ongoing process of looking at objectives from a developmental perspective. The early literacy continuums were designed to be a support for the ongoing process of developing and/or structuring assessments that provide valuable information about students' learning. They were designed as a support in providing more intentional learning experiences for students. They were designed as a support for informing parents and community members as to where their students are in their development as readers and writers, as well as where teachers, schools, or districts are in their understanding about teaching the youngest readers and writers. The early literacy continuums were designed to show the power and promise of developmentally appropriate assessment and instruction in the early primary years.

APS's Early Childhood Education Program is learning by doing. They are in the beginning stages of looking at how young children learn to read and write and how best to teach them. Because of the Early Literacy Continuum for Reading and Early Literacy Continuum for Writing, their preschools' faculties are making major shifts in how they approach teaching and learning, as well as how they collect data and record student growth. As a result, their preschool teachers are developing stronger understandings about assessment and evaluation, stronger theories of reading and writing, stronger understandings about their instructional resources, and stronger understandings of developmentally appropriate practices. Because these teachers are working to understand more about the craft of teaching young children, their students already have stronger foundations in early literacy and an increased capacity to meet the challenges of learning to read and write.

Appendix

Permission is granted to teachers and school districts to adapt this continuum for educational purposes only. Please credit as "The Early Literacy Continuum for Reading" © 2006 by Deborah K. Freeman and David M. Matteson. Published in Matteson, David M. and Deborah K. Freeman. *Assessing and Teaching Beginning Readers: A Picture is Worth 1000 Words.* Katonah, NY: Richard C. Owen Publishers, Inc., 2006. All rights reserved.

Early Literacy Continuum for Reading

Levels of Book-Handling Skills	Teaching Objectives[1]	Levels of Oral Language[2] (in the language of instruction)

Levels of Book-Handling Skills

1. The student's interactions with books reveal very few understandings about print in place. The book may be upside down or backwards. The student randomly flips through the pages and will go through several books in a short period of time.

2. The student's interactions with books reveal more understanding about print. The book is held right side up, and the reader goes from front to back. The reading still involves flipping through the pages, but the reader will spend more time looking at the pictures. The student may go through several books in a short period of time.

3. Basic understandings about print are secure. The student's interactions with books are more deliberate. The pace of reading is slowed by the reader's attention to pictures. The student picks out detail, but it may be random and *not critical* to the story.

4. The student's interactions with books show attention to the detail critical to the story but may ignore any print on the page.

5. The student's interactions with books show attention to detail critical to the story, and the student notices some print on the page.

Teaching Objectives[1]

Through individual pictures the student will be able to:
-
-
-
-

Through stories the student will be able to:
-
-
-
-
-
-
-

The student will be able to:
-
-

© 2006 by Deborah K. Freeman and David M. Mattteson

Levels of Oral Language[2] (in the language of instruction)

1. The student will not converse about the book. However, he or she may point or gesture.

2. The student names objects using words, short phrases, or simple sentences about the book through teacher questioning. However, the student may seem unsure of the story and/or give different responses during continued reading.

3. The student names objects using words, short phrases, or simple sentences about the book. The language and story remains constant during the reading and re-reading *over time*.

4. The student begins to tell a simple story about the book through teacher questioning.

5. The student is able to tell a story about the book with little or no teacher support.

[1]District and/or state goals and/or emergent characteristics are placed here.

[2]In ELL/ESL and bilingual classrooms, the teacher evaluates the student's performance in the language of instruction. For example, in a Spanish bilingual classroom, the language of instruction is Spanish. In any ELL/ESL classroom, the language of instruction is English.

References

Alborough, Jez. 2000. *Hug.* Cambridge, MA: Candlewick Press, Inc.

Allington, Richard L. and Patricia M. Cunningham. 1996. *Schools That Work: Where All Children Read and Write,* 1/e. New York, NY: HarperCollins.

Brown, Marc. 1997. *Where's Arthur's Gerbil?* New York, NY: Random House.

Calkins, Lucy McCormick. 2001. *The Art of Teaching Reading.* New York, NY: Addison-Wesley Educational Publishers, Inc.

Cambourne, Brian. 1988. *The Whole Story: Natural Learning and the Acquisition of Literacy in the Classroom.* Auckland, New Zealand: Ashton Scholastic Limited.

Clarke, Shirley. 2003. *Enriching Feedback in the Primary Classroom: Oral and Written Feedback from Teachers and Children.* London, UK: Hodder & Stoughton.

Clay, Marie M. 1991. *Becoming Literate: The Construction of Inner Control.* Portsmouth, NH: Heinemann.

Clay, Marie M. 1993. *An Observation Survey of Early Literacy Achievement.* Portsmouth, NH: Heinemann.

Clay, Marie M. 2001. *Change over Time in Children's Literacy Development.* Portsmouth, NH: Heinemann.

Cox, Rhonda. 1999. *Best Friends.* Katonah, NY: Richard C. Owen Publishers, Inc.

Duke, Nell K. 2003. "Reading to Learn from the Very Beginning: Information Books in Early Childhood." *Young Children.* Volume 58, number 2, March, pages 14-20.

Duke, Nell K. 2004. "The Case for Informational Text." *Educational Leadership.* Volume 61, number 6, March, pages 40-44.

Duncan, Marilyn. 2005. *The Kindergarten Book: A Guide to Literacy Instruction.* Katonah, NY: Richard C. Owen Publishers, Inc.

Fractor, J. S., M. C. Woodruff, M. G. Martinez, and W. H. Teale. 1993. "Let's Not Miss Opportunities to Promote Voluntary Reading: Classroom Libraries in the Elementary School." *The Reading Teacher.* Volume 46, number 6, March, pages 476-484.

Gaffney, Janet S. and Billie J. Askew, editors. 1999. *Stirring the Waters: The Influence of Marie Clay.* Portsmouth, NH: Heinemann.

Harwayne, Shelly. 1999. *Going Public: Priorities and Practices at The Manhattan New School.* Portsmouth, NH: Heinemann.

Hest, Amy. 2001. *Kiss Good Night.* Cambridge, MA: Candlewick Press.

Huck, Charlotte S. 1999. "The Gift of Story." In *Stirring the Waters: The Influence of Marie Clay,* edited by Janet S. Gaffney and Billie J. Askew. Portsmouth, NH: Heinemann.

International Reading Association. 2005. "Literacy Development in the Preschool Years: A Position Statement of the International Reading Association."

Llewellyn, Claire. 2005. *The Best Book of Sharks.* London, UK: Kingfisher.

Martin, Bill, Jr. 1996. *Brown Bear, Brown Bear, What Do You See?* New York, NY: Henry Holt.

Matteson, David M. 2005. *My Pictures and Stories: Teacher's Guide.* Katonah, NY: Richard C. Owen Publishers, Inc.

Matteson, David M. 2005. *My Pictures and Stories.* Katonah, NY: Richard C. Owen Publishers, Inc.

Matteson, David M. and Deborah K. Freeman. 2005. *Assessing and Teaching Beginning Writers: Every Picture Tells a Story.* Katonah, NY: Richard C. Owen Publishers, Inc.

Ministry of Education. 1985. *Reading in Junior Classes.* Wellington, New Zealand: School Publications Branch.

Ministry of Education. 1992. *Dancing with the Pen: The Learner as a Writer.* Wellington, New Zealand: Learning Media.

Ministry of Education. 1997. *Reading for Life: The Learner as a Reader.* Wellington, New Zealand: Learning Media.

Mooney, Margaret E. 1990. *Reading To, With, and By Children.* Katonah, NY: Richard C. Owen Publishers, Inc.

Mooney, Margaret E. 2001. *Text Forms and Features: A Resource for Intentional Teaching.* Katonah, NY: Richard C. Owen Publishers, Inc.

Mooney, Margaret. 1988. *Developing Life-long Readers.* Wellington, New Zealand: Learning Media.

Morrow, Lesley M. 2001. *Literacy Development in the Early Years: Helping Children Read and Write,* 4/e. Boston, MA: Allyn and Bacon.

Morrow, Lesley Mandel and Carol Simon Weinstein. 1986. "Encouraging Voluntary Reading: The Impact of a Literature Program on Children's Use of Library Centers." *Reading Research Quarterly.* Volume 21, number 3, Summer, pages 330-346.

National Association for the Education of Young Children. 1997. "Developmentally Appropriate Practice in Early Childhood Programs Serving Children from Birth through Age 8: A Position Statement of the NAEYC." Adopted July 1996. Washington, DC: © 1997 (NAEYC.org) position statement.

National Institute of Child Health and Human Development. 2000. Report of the National Reading Panel. Teaching children to read: An evidence-based assessment of the scientific research literature on reading and its implications for reading instruction (NIH Publication No. 00-4769). Washington, DC: U.S. Government Printing Office.

Neuman, Susan B., Carol Copple, and Sue Bredekamp. 2000. *Learning to Read and Write: Developmentally Appropriate Practices.* Washington, DC: National Association for the Education of Young Children.

Paley, Vivian Gussin. 1981. *Wally's Stories: Conversations in the Kindergarten.* Cambridge, MA: Harvard University Press.

Peck, Richard. 2005. "From the Desk of Richard Peck." *Dear Teacher: A Book of Days with Special Messages from Your Favorite Authors and Illustrators.* Unnumbered. Jefferson City, MO: Scholastic Book Clubs 2005-2006.

Sendak, Maurice. 1963. *Where the Wild Things Are.* New York, NY: HarperCollins.

Index

Academically rigorous, 50-51
Achievement of children, xvi, 49, 113
Advanced readers, 58
After reading, 26, 32, 49, 64, 83
Alborough, Jez, xii, 13, 16, 84, 126
Aligning reading and writing, 97-98, 99
Allington, Richard L., 30, 126
Approximating, 11, 40, 56, 59, 62
Assessing and Teaching Beginning Writers: Every Picture Tells a Story (Matteson and Freeman), ix, xii, xvii, 97, 131
Assessments, 97, 99, 104-112, 113-114, 116-117, 119, 121, 123
Atmosphere, 27, 49, 96
Attending, 7, 60, 86, 90, 97, 103, 111
Attention to detail, xvi, 3, 65, 85, 88, 97, 102-103, 112, 114
Attitudes about reading, 11
Attitudes of writers, 95
Aural language, 2-3, 6-7
Aural skills, 1, 4
Aurora Public School's Preschool Continuum, xv-xvii, 102, 112, 113, 122
Author, 14, 16, 29, 40, 72, 73
Average of the class, 114, 117

Before reading, 14, 67-69, 72, 79, 104
Beginning of story, 7, 26
Beginning reading, 39, 40
    comprehension, 1-9
    instruction, vii, ix, xiii, xvi, 34
Beginning writer, 93
Beginning writing instruction, 85, 102
Behaviors as writers, 88, 89
Behaviors as readers, ix-xii, 3, 26, 28, 36, 43, 46, 88
    list of, 5
    monitoring, 99-112
Beliefs, 36
Best Book of Sharks, The (Llewellyn), 56, 66, 110, 111, 112, 130

Best Friends (Cox), xii, 68, 69-83, 130
Book-handling skill graph, 118
Book-handling skills, x-xi, 65, 85, 100, 102, 104-107, 110, 117-121
    levels, 100, 120
Bookmarks, 16, 46, 64, 65
Books, knowing how they work, 3, 6, 88
Bredekamp, Sue, 132
Brown, Marc, 39, 129

Calkins, Lucy M., 113, 129
Cambourne, Brian, 11
Caregivers, vii, 50
"Case for Informational Text, The" (Duke), 54, 130
Characteristics of emergent readers, 4-5, 6, 8
Characteristics of emergent writers, 88-90
Children at risk, 53
Chunks of language, 3, 87
Clarke, Shirley, 99
Classroom library, 27-28, 35, 64, 66, 68, 92, 108, 110, 111, 132
Classroom setup, 27, 28, 31-33
Clay, Marie, 8, 87, 129, 130
Cognitive concepts, 1-2
Collecting data, 98
Comprehension, xiii, 1-9, 27, 42, 44, 51, 54, 83, 85, 88
    strategies, 54
    teaching, 69-83
Confidence, 11, 67, 93, 95, 122
Confirmation, vii, 9, 16, 41, 45
Connections
    of oral language and pictures, ix, 13, 88
    between reading and writing, 88, 102, 112
    to stories by reader, 44, 50, 96, 116
    within story structure, 7, 12, 21, 55
    of text and pictures, 24
Containers, use of, 30-31, 55
Content knowledge, 64

Continuum in action, 103-106
Conversations, vii-viii, 9, 21, 49, 94, 102, 121
Coordination, 8
Copple, Carol, 132
Corrections, 63, 89
Cover of book, v, 14-15, 39, 56, 71-72, 79, 81, 82, 90, 104
Cox, Rhonda, xii, 69, 73, 84, 130
Creating meaning, 2
Critical, xi, 19, 23, 28, 102, 111, 127
Cunningham, Patricia M., 30, 129

Dancing with the Pen: The Learner as a Writer (Ministry of Education), 90, 131
Decisions, 6, 22, 97, 112, 117, 121, 122
Decoding, 87-88
Deeper understanding, 71, 72, 79
Demonstration, xii, xvi, 116
   role of, 11-26
Description, 7, 50, 66, 78, 94, 103, 111
Descriptive phrases, 12, 50
Detail, 13, 14
Developing Life-long Readers (Mooney), 3, 131
Developmental levels, 97, 100
Developmentally appropriate, ix, xiii, 6, 9, 51, 123, 132
Diagrams, 7, 55, 60
Dialogue, viii, 7, 50, 67, 78, 96, 103-104
Difficult texts, 68
Discussion, 13, 15, 42, 72, 74
Dramatic play, 1, 9
Duke, Nell, 53, 54, 130
Duncan, Marilyn, 11, 130
During reading, 13. *See also* Vignettes

Early childhood teachers, 26, 49, 51
Early literacy intervention, 87

Early Literacy Continuum for Reading, xii, xv, xvi-xvii, 97, 98, 99, 100-103, 112, 113-114, 119, 122, 123, 125-127
   blank, 127
   sample, 101
Early Literacy Continuum for Writing, xv, xvi, 97, 99, 112, 122, 123
Early primary grades, 3, 9
Emergent readers, xi, 28, 121
   characteristics of, 3, 4-5, 6, 8, 88
Emergent writers, characteristics of, 88-90, 93
Encoding, 87, 88
End of story, 7, 26, 55
Engagement, 25
Environment, xv, 3, 9, 35, 36
Evaluation, xv, xvi, 123
Expectations, 28-29
Exploring books, vii, 53
Expository elements, 7, 96
Expression, 1, 4, 5, 13, 40, 45, 46, 88, 89, 95

Fiction, 7, 30-32
Flipping through books, 12, 100, 103, 105
Fluency, 42
Fluent readers, 33
Focused topic, 7, 55
Formal reading instruction, 51
Foundations, vii, x, xvi, 2, 3, 36, 50-51, 85, 123
Fractor, J. S., 29
Freeman, Deborah K., ix, xii, 97, 99, 101, 102, 113, 127

Genre, 7, 29, 51, 54, 110, 112
Graphing, 114-115
Graphs, sample, 115, 118, 119, 120
Grouping, xi, 11, 65, 67, 69, 116, 117, 121

Growth over time, 91
Guided reading, 11

Harwayne, Shelly, 31, 130
Hearing, 12, 33
Hest, Amy, 103, 130
Higher levels of comprehension, 83
Huck, Charlotte S., 37, 130
HUG (Alborough), xii, 14-25, 26, 34, 126

Illustrations. *See* Pictures
Independent reading, 12, 68
Inferences, 46
Informational text, xii, 31, 32, 51, 54
   monitoring reading of, 65-66
   playing at reading, 55-65
Instructional connections, 99
Instructional decisions, 97, 117, 121
Intentional teaching, ix-x, 1-3, 22, 24-26,
   55, 68
Internalized understanding, 49
International Reading Association (IRA),
   3, 130
Interrelatedness of reading and writing,
   87-98
Intonation, 19, 25, 47, 60, 109, 110
Introduction. *See* Before reading

Key words, 7, 55, 90
Kiss Good Night (Hest), 103, 108, 130

Labeled diagrams, 60
Language style, 12, 17
Leveled book boxes, 68
Levels
   of book-handling skills, 100, 120
   of oral language, 97, 100, 114, 115, 119,
   120
   student work, 115, 121

Library, xii, 6, 12, 26, 27-36, 51, 53-55, 64-
   65, 67-68, 70, 103, 104, 107, 117, 132.
   See also Classroom library
Listening skills, 1, 4, 7, 33, 35, 79, 96
Literacy development, v, 3, 9, 36, 51, 96,
   97, 98, 99, 129, 130, 131
Literacy instruction, ix, 3, 130
Literal level, 68, 83
Literate homes, 36, 37, 38, 49, 51
Literature collections, 27
Llewellyn, Claire, 56, 130
Lower reading levels, 83

Making meaning, 56, 83, 109
Matteson, David M., viii, ix, xii, 91, 97, 99,
   102, 113, 125, 131
Memory for text, 5, 67, 109, 110
Messages carrying meaning, 26, 71, 87,
   90, 93, 95, 103
Middle of story, 7, 26
Ministry of Education, 35, 90
Modeling, 12, 13, 26, 31, 46, 54, 74, 83
Monitoring, 43, 55, 97, 109-112, 113, 115,
   122
   attention to detail, xvi, 3, 65, 85, 88, 97,
   102, 103, 112, 114
   informational text, reading of, 65-66
   notes, 65, 66, 108, 109, 110, 111, 112
   levels, 97, 100, 114, 115, 119, 120
   oral language, 96, 112, 115, 117
Mooney, Margaret, vii-viii, xi, 5, 11, 55, 131
Morrow, Lesley M., 27, 28, 131-132
My Pictures and Stories (Matteson), xvi,
   90, 91, 131

Narrative elements, 6, 7, 51, 94, 96
National Association for the Education of
   Young Children (NAEYC), 9

National Institute of Child Health and Human Development, 87
Next learning steps, 66, 97, 108, 110, 111. *See also* Planning
Next steps, 66, 108, 110, 111
Nonfiction, 7, 31-32
Noticing detail, 12, 88. *See also* Pictures, attending to detail in
Neuman, Susan B., 132

Objectives, x, 26, 55, 97, 102, 116
One-to-one matching, 67
Opportunities for discussion, 74
Oral language
   levels, 97, 100, 114, 115, 119, 120
   monitoring, 96, 112, 115, 117
   skills, 1, 4, 96
Organizational tools, 29

Paley, Vivian Gussin, 67, 132
Parents, v, ix, xii, 38, 39, 44, 47, 49, 50, 121, 123
Peck, Richard, 132
Perseverance, 47
Phrases, 12, 17, 18, 25, 40, 50, 100
Picture book, 15, 22, 37, 49, 103
Pictures
   attending to, 5, 13, 58, 60, 68, 107
   attending to detail in, xi, 3, 7, 59, 78, 102, 109
   differentiating from text, xi, 4, 57, 109, 111
   interacting with, 1, 2, 12, 61, 105
   using to make meaning, iv, xi, 2, 12, 46, 56, 68, 69, 74, 103, 108
   using to predict or support text, 5, 7, 14, 24, 41, 55, 60, 62, 66, 70, 79, 117

   using as source of information, 28, 29, 63, 70.
   See also Characteristics of emergent writers; Early Literacy Continuum for Reading; Wordless books
Planning, 12, 55, 68, 116, 117, 118
Playing at reading, v, vii-viii, 3-9, 12, 26, 27, 38, 40, 42, 43, 46, 51, 54, 55, 65, 92, 97, 100, 108, 109, 110
Position statement, 8, 9, 130-132
Practice of teachers, 8, 39, 65, 109, 121, 123
Practicing skills, 26, 32, 51, 55, 65, 68, 96, 110
Prediction, 5, 9, 16, 19, 21, 70, 79, 88, 106, 116, 117
Prekindergarten, ix, xii, 3, 27, 51, 98
Preschool, xiii, xv, 8, 9, 12, 120, 122, 123
   curriculum, 8
   literacy, 8
Presenting, 96
Print, 5, 6, 8, 9, 66, 106, 108, 109, 111
   awareness component, 102
   concepts, xi, 6, 40, 100
   holds meaning, 59, 89, 93
Professional development, 121, 122
Problem solving, 2, 3
Prompts, 83, 106, 107, 108. *See also* Questioning by teacher
Publishing student writing, 53, 93, 95
Puppet theater, 34

Questioning
   by student, 31, 44, 72, 79, 89
   by teacher, xi, 13, 26, 49, 69, 97, 107. *See also* Planning

Reading beyond words, 68, 83

Read-aloud, 31, 33. *See also*
  Documentation
Reading
  Aligning with writing, 90, 93, 94, 96-98,
    100
  Buddy, 56
  See also Beginning reading; Behaviors
    as readers; Early Literacy Continuum
    for Reading; Playing at reading
  group, 62-85
  proficiency, 39-51
  silently, 69
Reading for Life (Ministry of Education),
  35, 131
Receptive language, 1, 4, 5
Reciprocal process, 87-88
Relationships, 9, 90, 97
Relative independence, 87
Repetition, vii, 7, 18, 41, 43, 46, 55
Report of the National Reading Panel,
  132
Research, 8, 53, 64
Resources, 9, 31, 123
Retelling, 4, 9, 18, 32, 42, 96
Return sweep, 67
Risk taking, 11
Role of print, 107

Searching, 62, 66, 111
Self-confidence, 93
Self-correcting, 43
Self-stick notes, 24, 92, 93, 95
Semi-wordless books, 83, 84
Sense, making, 4, 41, 43, 44, 62
Sensory detail, 7, 50, 78, 94
Sentence structures, 60, 63, 66, 111
Setting, xv, 17, 50, 72, 78, 103
Shared reading, vii, 11

Sight vocabulary, 67
Significant event, 7, 50, 78
Small groups, xii, 9, 11, 51, 65
  reading in, 67-85
Sounding right, 43
Sound/letter correspondence, 56
Speech bubble, 14
Stopping points, 19, 74
Story development, 68, 74
Story reading, 9
Story telling, 9
Storybook language, 12, 17
Strengths, 6, 66, 108, 110, 111, 120
Strong connections, 24, 84, 88, 102
Structure of story, 3, 6, 88, 95
Student work, levels of, 115, 121
Support, 11, 12, 26, 30-32, 36, 38, 50, 51,
  53
Surface level, 12

Table of contents, 7, 55, 56, 57, 58, 111,
  112
Tapes, xii, 33
Teacher's intention, 69
Teacher-student interaction, 90, 107
Teacher talk, 19, 21
Teaching approach, 11, 13, 51
Teaching objectives, x, 97, 102, 116
Teaching points, 26, 55
*Text Forms and Features: A Resource for
  Intentional Teaching* (Mooney), 55,
  131
Text selection, 13, 29, 30, 54, 68
Text talk, 19, 21
Theme, x, 7, 50, 71, 72, 74, 78, 83, 103
Thinking, 3, 12, 37, 70, 72, 78, 79, 83, 96
Third grade, 83
Title page, v, 15, 16, 57, 66, 71

Titles
    consistency of, 16, 57
    introducing as text element, 14, 69, 109,
        111
    self-explanatory, 7, 55
    understandings about, 39, 56, 66, 105,
        108
    use of, 14, 66, 72
Total scores for book-handling skills, 118
Total scores for oral language, 115

Understandings about reading, 3, 4, 11,
    22, 34
Understandings about writing, 88, 89, 93

Vignettes, xii-xiii, 14-25, 39-49, 56-64, 69-
    83, 91-95, 104-107
Visual detail, 8

Vocabulary, vii, 7, 9, 12, 22, 23, 41, 55, 67,
    111

Weekly data collection, 91
Where the Wild Things Are (Sendak), 37,
    132
Where's Arthur's Gerbil? (Brown), 39, 40,
    110
Whole group, 11, 64, 116
Wordless books, 24, 65, 68, 74, 83-85. *See
    also Best Friends*
Writing, 11, 34, 49, 53, 64, 67, 85, 87, 87-
    95, 99
Writing book, 91
Writing conference, 91, 95
Writing instruction, 85, 88, 95, 99, 102
Written language, 9, 88